Letts
gets you through

D1633325

AQA GCSE 9-1

ENGLISH LANGUAGE AND LITERATURE

PRACTICE TEST PAPERS

GCSE

PAUL BURNS

Contents

English Language

English Literature

Acknowledgements

The author and publisher are grateful to the copyright holders for permission to use quoted materials and images.

'Bayonet Charge' from *Hawk in the Rain* by Ted Hughes, Faber & Faber

'Eden Rock' from *Collected Poems* by Charles Causley, reprinted by permission of David Higham Associates

'Winter Swans' from *Skirris Hill* by Owen Sheers, reprinted by permission of Rogers, Coleridge and White Ltd

'Remains' from *The Not Dead* by Simon Armitage, reprinted by permission of Pomona Books

Images are © Shutterstock.com

Every effort has been made to trace copyright holders and obtain their permission for the use of copyright material. The author and publisher will gladly receive information enabling them to rectify any error or omission in subsequent editions. All facts are correct at time of going to press.

Published by Letts Educational
An imprint of HarperCollins*Publishers*
1 London Bridge Street
London SE1 9GF

ISBN: 9780008276157

First published 2018

10 9 8 7 6 5 4 3

© HarperCollins*Publishers* Limited

British Library Cataloguing in Publication Data.

A CIP record of this book is available from the British Library.

Commissioning Editor: Clare Souza
Author: Paul Burns
Project Management and Editorial: Charlotte Christensen
Cover Design: Amparo Barrera
Inside Concept Design: Paul Oates
Production: Natalia Rebow
Text Design and Layout: Contentra Technologies
Printed and bound by CPI Group (UK) Ltd, Croydon, CR0 4YY

English Language Practice Papers Set A

Pages 4–7: English Language Paper 1: Explorations in Creative Reading and Writing

The questions on pages 4–7 will help you to revise for:

- AQA Paper 1: Explorations in Creative Reading and Writing

The marks for the questions are shown in square brackets.

There are 40 marks for Section A (reading) and 40 marks for Section B (writing). The maximum mark for this paper is 80.

Pages 8–12: English Language Paper 2: Writers' Viewpoints and Perspectives

The questions on pages 8–12 will help you to revise for:

- AQA Paper 2: Writers' Viewpoints and Perspectives

The marks for the questions are shown in square brackets.

There are 40 marks for Section A (reading) and 40 marks for Section B (writing). The maximum mark for this paper is 80.

Name: ....

English Language Paper 1:
Explorations in Creative Reading and Writing

- **You are advised to spend about 15 minutes reading through the source and all five questions.**
- **You should make sure you leave sufficient time to check your answers.**

Section A: Reading

Answer all questions in this section.

You are advised to spend about 45 minutes on this section.

Source This extract is the opening of 'Home Sickness', a short story by George Moore, first published in 1903. The story opens in New York.

He told the doctor he was due in the bar-room at eight o'clock in the morning; the bar-room was in a slum in the Bowery; and he had only been able to keep himself in health by getting up at five o'clock and going for long walks in the Central Park.

"A sea voyage is what you want," said the doctor. "Why not go to Ireland for two or three
5 months? You will come back a new man."

"I'd like to see Ireland again."

And he began to wonder how the people at home were getting on. The doctor was right. He thanked him, and three weeks afterwards he landed in Cork.

As he sat in the railway carriage he recalled his native village, built among the rocks of the
10 large headland stretching out into the winding lake. He could see the houses and the streets, and the fields of the tenants, and the Georgian mansion and the owners of it; he and they had been boys together before he went to America. He remembered the villagers going every morning to the big house to work in the stables, in the garden, in the fields - mowing, reaping, digging, and Michael Malia building a wall; it was all as clear as if it were yesterday, yet he had
15 been thirteen years in America; and when the train stopped at the station, the first thing he did was to look round for any changes that might have come into it. It was the same blue limestone station as it was thirteen years ago, with the same five long miles between it and Duncannon. He had once walked these miles gaily, in a little over an hour, carrying a heavy bundle on a stick, but he did not feel strong enough for the walk today, though the evening tempted him
20 to try it. A car[1] was waiting at the station, and the boy, discerning from his accent and his dress that Bryden had come from America, plied him with questions, which Bryden answered rapidly, for he wanted to hear who were still living in the village, and if there was a house in which he could get a clean lodging. The best house in the village, he was told, was Mike Scully's, who had been away in a situation for many years, as a coachman in the King's County, but had come back
25 and built a fine house with a concrete floor. The boy could recommend the loft, he had slept in it himself, and Mike would be glad to take in a lodger, he had no doubt. Bryden remembered that Mike had been in a situation at the Big House. He had intended to be a jockey, but had suddenly shot up into a fine tall man, and had had to become a coachman instead; and Bryden

tried to recall the face, but he could only remember a straight nose, and a somewhat dusky
30 complexion.

So Mike had come back from King's County, and had built himself a house, had married –
there were children for sure running about; while he, Bryden, had gone to America, but he had
come back; perhaps he, too, would build a house in Duncannon, and – his reverie was suddenly
interrupted by the carman.

35 "There's Mike Scully," he said, pointing with his whip, and Bryden saw a tall, finely-built,
middle-aged man coming through the gates, who looked astonished when he was accosted, for he
had forgotten Bryden even more completely than Bryden had forgotten him; and many aunts and
uncles were mentioned before he began to understand.

"You've grown into a fine man, James," he said, looking at Bryden's great width of chest. "But
40 you're thin in the cheeks, and you're very sallow in the cheeks too."

"I haven't been well lately - that is one of the reasons I've come back; but I want to see you all
again."

"And thousand welcome you are."

¹car – here a cab, drawn by a horse, for hire like a taxi

1. Read again the first part of the source from lines 1 to 8. List four things about Bryden ('he') from this part of the source.

1 he was due in the bar-room at eight o'clock in the morning.

2 he had only be able to keep himself in health by getting up at 5'oclock.

3 he landed in Cork

4 he began to wonder how people at home were getting [4 marks] on.

2. Look in detail at this extract from lines 9 to 16 of the source.

> As he sat in the railway carriage he recalled his native village, built among the rocks of the large headland stretching out into the winding lake. He could see the houses and the streets, and the fields of the tenants, and the Georgian mansion and the owners of it; he and they had been boys together before he went to America. He remembered the villagers going every morning to the big house to work in the stables, in the garden, in the fields - mowing, reaping, digging, and Michael Malia building a wall; it was all as clear as if it were yesterday, yet he had been thirteen years in America; and when the train stopped at the station, the first thing he did was to look round for any changes that might have come into it.

How does the writer use language here to create an impression of life in Duncannon?

You could include the writer's choice of:
- words and phrases
- language features and techniques
- sentence forms.

[8 marks]

3. You now need to think about the **whole** of the source.

This text is from the beginning of a short story.

How has the writer structured the text to interest you as a reader?

You could write about:
- what the writer focuses your attention on at the beginning of the source
- how and why the writer changes this focus as the source develops
- any other structural features that interest you.   **[8 marks]**

4. Focus this part of your answer on the second part of the source, from line 16 to the end.

A student said, 'In James Bryden, the writer has created a character that readers can sympathise with. We really want to know the outcome of his return to Ireland.'

How far do you agree?
- Write about your own impressions of James Bryden and his return to Ireland.
- Evaluate how the writer has created these impressions.
- Support your opinions with quotations from the text.   **[20 marks]**

Section B: Writing

You are advised to spend about 45 minutes on this section.

You are reminded of the need to plan your answer.

You should write in full sentences.

You should leave enough time to check your work at the end.

5. A national magazine is running a creative writing competition and intends to publish the winning entries.

EITHER

(a) Write a description of a place suggested by this picture.

OR

(b) Write a story that begins 'I sat on the park bench and thought about what the doctor had said.'

[24 marks for content and organisation and 16 marks for technical accuracy; total 40 marks]

END OF QUESTIONS

English Language Paper 2: Writers' Viewpoints and Perspectives

- **You are advised to spend about 15 minutes reading through the sources and all five questions.**
- **You should make sure you leave sufficient time to check your answers.**

Section A: Reading

Answer all questions in this section.

You are advised to spend about 45 minutes on this section.

Source A is an extract from *The Food of London,* by George Dodd, published in 1856. In this chapter, the writer describes how bread is made in London and compares it to what is happening in Paris and Birmingham.

The bread-making processes are, indeed, clumsily managed in the majority of London establishments. Whoever has seen the rude and primitive mode in which dough is kneaded, by a man straddling and wriggling on the end of a lever or pole, may well marvel that such uncouthness should not long ago have been superseded by something better. Our Parisian neighbours appear to be somewhat in the same plight as
5 ourselves. On a recent occasion, M. Payen, a distinguished French chemist, made a Report to the Academie Française on the bread and baking of Paris. He said: "A day will doubtless come when our descendants, who shall read the technology of the 19th century, will ask themselves whether at this time of industrial progress we really prepared the chief of our aliments by the rude way which we now witness – in plunging the arms into the dough, lifting it up and crushing it down with such effort as to exhaust the energy of the half-naked
10 arms, and make the perspiration run down into the food; whether at such an epoch the baking was effected on the very hearth itself from whence the fuel had just been withdrawn; whether it could be believed that during these fatiguing operations the chief part of the heat should seem destined to heat, or rather to roast, the workmen, than to bake the bread!" The Parisian practice is tolerably well marked out in this passage; but improvements seem to be in progress. A committee of the Academie, MM. Payen, Poncelet, and Boussingault,
15 have reported in high terms on a system invented and patented by M. Rolland, in which a kneading machine, worked by hand, will knead a sack of flour into dough in 20 minutes, with a vast saving of muscular labour.

It is strange that, in the greatest city in the world, we have nothing that can be called a large bread-factory. Steam-mills there are on a gigantic scale, as has already been noticed; biscuit-bakeries, in which steam-power is employed to mix and knead the dough; bakers who make frequent changes and improvements in
20 their ovens; but no establishment wherein the plain familiar four pound loaf is made by machinery.

[…] There are now six large bread mills in Birmingham … At one of the largest of these mills, belonging to Mr Lucy, lately Mayor of Birmingham, steam-worked cranes haul up the sacks of wheat from a canal of granaries at the top of the building; steam works fourteen pairs of millstones to grind the corn; steam mixes the wheat before grinding, and the flour after grinding; steam kneads the flour, and water,
25 and yeast, and salt into well-made dough; and then come the manipulative processes. The bakehouse has tables of large size, and around its walls are eight ovens of great capacity. The dough is made into loaves; the loaves are nicely baked in the ovens; and the baked bread is placed on shelves in a storeroom which will contain 2000 loaves. The mill sells flour as well as bread. At an early hour in the mornings waggons draw up to the mill; they are filled with loaves, which are quickly conveyed to the several hucksters'
30 shops[1], and the waggoner, or attendant servant, returns with the ready money. The huckster sells the bread to the families of the working men of Birmingham.

[1]Hucksters' shops — shops that sell a variety of goods cheaply

Source B is an advertising feature for a local bakery.

Archie's Artisan Bakery

Welcome!

Here at Archie's Artisan Bakery, we're putting baking back into the heart of the community. Step into our village bakery and you'll be greeted by the smell of freshly baked bread - a smell that says 'home' - and the sight of a dazzling array of breads,
5 *pastries and cakes.*

Archie and Fab

Hi, I'm Archie Bold, the co-owner of Archie's Artisan Bakery, and the master baker. I'm a local lad, coming from a long line of bakers and confectioners. After attending a local catering
10 college and spending a year as a sous chef at a Michelin starred London restaurant, I felt the family trade calling. But I was also aware of how many of the traditional skills have been lost here in Britain. To get the best possible training, I took myself off to France, where I trained with some of the world's best artisan
15 bakers.

I also fell in love, not just with French baking but with *maîtresse patissiere*, 'Fab' Fabienne Rollard. Five years later we're married and I've fulfilled my childhood dream by opening my own bakery in the beautiful village of Rotterthwaite, just ten miles from my hometown.

20 Today, Fab's fabulous choux pastry creations bring a touch of Parisian sophistication to our village bakery, sitting happily alongside more traditional British cakes, many inspired by old family recipes.

Real Bread!

What do we mean by real bread? Well, we don't mean white sliced pre-packaged bread, full of additives and made on an industrial scale in huge factories. Nor do we mean the bread that you might find in your local supermarket, supposedly 'baked on the premises' when in fact it has been half-baked somewhere else, driven miles in a van to your local store and then 'finished off' quickly.

Real bread - or artisan bread as it's often called - is made with just four things: flour, water, salt and yeast.

In France, a shop can only call itself a *boulangerie* if all five processes involved in bread making - fermentation, mixing, kneading, shaping and baking - happen in the one place. We don't have that rule in Britain, but that's exactly what happens at Archie's. And it's all done by hand.

I believe that real bread is more than food for the body - it's food for the soul. My assistants, Stan and Rita, and I bring years of experience and expertise to our craft. We also bring passion and love. A real baker bakes not just with the head and the hands, but with the heart.

How We Make Our Bread

For us, local ingredients are key. We source our ingredients locally wherever possible. Our top quality organic flour, for example, comes from Gorton's Mills just thirty miles down the road. The bread-making process starts with 'starter', created from flour and water and natural yeast - wild yeasts for our increasingly popular sourdough range.

A good loaf takes many hours to create. And a good baker needs patience as well as skill and flair.

After we've shaped our loaves and allowed them to gently rise, they are baked in our traditional oven.

In this way, we can produce over 200 top quality loaves of the finest artisan breads each day - sourdoughs, baguettes, wholemeal, crusty white, granary and even gluten-free.

Visit Us!

We are open from Monday to Saturday between 8.30 a.m. and 5.00 p.m. and you're welcome to visit and see us at work whenever the shop is open. We'll even show you round the bakery and share some of our secrets.

We also have a local delivery service and you can order your bread and cakes the day before you want them, either online, by telephone or just by popping into the shop. Keep in touch with us via our website where you'll find full details (and mouth-watering pictures!) of all our delicious products.

1. Read again Source A from lines 1 to 16.

   Choose four statements below that are TRUE.
   - Shade the boxes of the ones that you think are true.
   - Choose a maximum of four statements.

   A. Bakers in London and Paris make bread in a similar way. ☐

   B. M. Payen is a biologist. ☐

   C. The writer thinks all bread should be made by hand. ☐

   D. M. Rolland has invented a machine for kneading dough. ☐

   E. M. Payen has written a novel about bakers in Paris. ☐

   F. Most of the heat from the Paris bread ovens is wasted. ☐

   G. Making bread is physically hard work. ☐

   H. The committee of the Academie Française was not impressed by Rolland's system. ☐

   [4 marks]

2. You need to refer to Source A and Source B for this question.

   Use details from both sources. Write a summary of the differences between Lucy's bread mill and Archie's Artisan Bakery. **[8 marks]**

3. You now need to refer only to Source B, the advertising feature for Archie's Artisan Bakery.

   How does the writer use language to try to engage and influence the reader? **[12 marks]**

4. For this question, you need to refer to both Source A and Source B.

   Compare how the writers convey different attitudes to bread-making.

   In your answer you should:
   - compare the different attitudes
   - compare the methods they use to convey these attitudes
   - support your ideas with references to both texts. **[16 marks]**

Section B: Writing

You are advised to spend about 45 minutes on this section.

You are reminded of the need to plan your answer.

You should write in full sentences.

You should leave enough time to check your work at the end.

5. 'It's all very well for celebrity TV chefs to go on about healthy eating and not buying convenience food, but when you're working hard and managing on a budget, you simply haven't got the time or energy to follow their advice.'

Write an article for a newspaper on which you argue for or against this statement.

[24 marks for content and organisation and 16 marks for technical accuracy; total 40 marks]

END OF QUESTIONS

English Language Practice Papers Set B

Pages 14–18: English Language Paper 1: Explorations in Creative Reading and Writing

The questions on pages 14–18 will help you to revise for:

• AQA Paper 1: Explorations in Creative Reading and Writing

The marks for the questions are shown in square brackets.

There are 40 marks for Section A (reading) and 40 marks for Section B (writing). The maximum mark for this paper is 80.

Pages 19–22: English Language Paper 2: Writers' Viewpoints and Perspectives

The questions on pages 19–22 will help you to revise for:

• AQA Paper 2: Writers' Viewpoints and Perspectives

The marks for the questions are shown in square brackets.

There are 40 marks for Section A (reading) and 40 marks for Section B (writing). The maximum mark for this paper is 80.

Name: ....

English Language Paper 1:
Explorations in Creative Reading and Writing

- **You are advised to spend about 15 minutes reading through the source and all five questions.**
- **You should make sure you leave sufficient time to check your answers.**

Section A: Reading

Answer all questions in this section.

You are advised to spend about 45 minutes on this section.

Source The text is a complete short story, 'The Story of an Hour', by Kate Chopin, first published in 1894.

Knowing that Mrs. Mallard was afflicted with a heart trouble, great care was taken to break to her as gently as possible the news of her husband's death.

It was her sister Josephine who told her, in broken sentences; veiled hints that revealed in half concealing. Her husband's friend Richards was there, too, near her. It was he who had been in the newspaper office when intelligence of the railroad disaster was received, with Brently Mallard's name leading the list of "killed." He had only taken the time to assure himself of its truth by a second telegram, and had hastened to forestall any less careful, less tender friend in bearing the sad message.

She did not hear the story as many women have heard the same, with a paralyzed inability to accept its significance. She wept at once, with sudden, wild abandonment, in her sister's arms. When the storm of grief had spent itself she went away to her room alone. She would have no one follow her.

There stood, facing the open window, a comfortable, roomy armchair. Into this she sank, pressed down by a physical exhaustion that haunted her body and seemed to reach into her soul.

She could see in the open square before her house the tops of trees that were all aquiver with the new spring life. The delicious breath of rain was in the air. In the street below a peddler was crying his wares. The notes of a distant song which someone was singing reached her faintly, and countless sparrows were twittering in the eaves.

There were patches of blue sky showing here and there through the clouds that had met and piled one above the other in the west facing her window.

She sat with her head thrown back upon the cushion of the chair, quite motionless, except when a sob came up into her throat and shook her, as a child who has cried itself to sleep continues to sob in its dreams.

She was young, with a fair, calm face, whose lines bespoke repression and even a certain strength. But now there was a dull stare in her eyes, whose gaze was fixed away off yonder on one of those patches of blue sky. It was not a glance of reflection, but rather indicated a suspension of intelligent thought.

There was something coming to her and she was waiting for it, fearfully. What was it? She did not know; it was too subtle and elusive to name. But she felt it, creeping out of the sky, reaching toward her through the sounds, the scents, the color that filled the air.

Now her bosom rose and fell tumultuously. She was beginning to recognize this thing that was approaching to possess her, and she was striving to beat it back with her will – as powerless as her two white slender hands would have been.

When she abandoned herself a little whispered word escaped her slightly parted lips. She said it over and over under her breath: "Free, free, free!" The vacant stare and the look of terror that had followed it went from her eyes. They stayed keen and bright. Her pulses beat fast, and the coursing blood warmed and relaxed every inch of her body.

She did not stop to ask if it were or were not a monstrous joy that held her. A clear and exalted perception enabled her to dismiss the suggestion as trivial.

She knew that she would weep again when she saw the kind, tender hands folded in death; the face that had never looked save with love upon her, fixed and gray and dead. But she saw beyond that bitter moment a long procession of years to come that would belong to her absolutely. And she opened and spread her arms out to them in welcome.

There would be no one to live for during those coming years; she would live for herself. There would be no powerful will bending hers in that blind persistence with which men and women believe they have a right to impose a private will upon a fellow-creature. A kind intention or a cruel intention made the act seem no less a crime as she looked upon it in that brief moment of illumination.

And yet she had loved him – sometimes. Often she had not. What did it matter! What could love, the unsolved mystery, count for in the face of this possession of self-assertion which she suddenly recognized as the strongest impulse of her being!

"Free! Body and soul free!" she kept whispering.

Josephine was kneeling before the closed door with her lips to the keyhole, imploring for admission.

"Louise, open the door! I beg; open the door – you will make yourself ill. What are you doing, Louise? For heaven's sake open the door."

"Go away. I am not making myself ill." No; she was drinking in a very elixir of life through that open window.

Her fancy was running riot along those days ahead of her. Spring days, and summer days, and all sorts of days that would be her own. She breathed a quick prayer that life might be long. It was only yesterday she had thought with a shudder that life might be long.

She arose at length and opened the door to her sister's importunities. There was a feverish triumph in her eyes, and she carried herself unwittingly like a goddess of Victory. She clasped her sister's waist, and together they descended the stairs. Richards stood waiting for them at the bottom.

Someone was opening the front door with a latchkey. It was Brently Mallard who entered, a little travel-stained, composedly carrying his grip-sack and umbrella. He had been far from the scene of the accident, and did not even know there had been one. He stood amazed at Josephine's piercing cry; at Richards' quick motion to screen him from the view of his wife.

But Richards was too late.

When the doctors came they said she had died of heart disease – of joy that kills.

1. Read again lines 13 to 18 of the source.

List four things that Louise Mallard can see or hear through the window.

1 ....

2 ....

3 ....

4 .... **[4 marks]**

2. Look in detail at this extract from lines 22 to 31 of the source.

> She was young, with a fair, calm face, whose lines bespoke repression and even a certain strength. But now there was a dull stare in her eyes, whose gaze was fixed away off yonder on one of those patches of blue sky. It was not a glance of reflection, but rather indicated a suspension of intelligent thought.
>
> There was something coming to her and she was waiting for it, fearfully. What was it? She did not know; it was too subtle and elusive to name. But she felt it, creeping out of the sky, reaching toward her through the sounds, the scents, the color that filled the air.
>
> Now her bosom rose and fell tumultuously. She was beginning to recognize this thing that was approaching to possess her, and she was striving to beat it back with her will – as powerless as her two white slender hands would have been.

How does the writer use language here to describe Louise Mallard's state of mind at this point in the story?

You could include the writer's choice of:
- words and phrases
- language features and techniques
- sentence forms. **[8 marks]**

3. You now need to think about the **whole** of the source.

This text is a complete short story.

How has the writer structured the story to interest you as a reader?

You could write about:
- what the writer focuses your attention on at the beginning
- how and why she changes this focus as the source develops
- any other structural features that interest you.

[8 marks]

4. Focus this part of your answer on the second part of the source, from line 19 to the end.

A student said, 'The writer uses Louise Mallard to express very negative views about marriage'.

To what extent do you agree?

In your response you could:
- consider your own impressions of Louise's feelings
- evaluate how the writer conveys ideas about, and attitudes to, marriage
- support your response with references to the text.

[20 marks]

Section B: Writing

5. A local newspaper is running a writing competition. The winning entries will be published.

EITHER

(a) Describe a day out as suggested by this picture.

OR

(b) Write a story about someone whose life changes suddenly.

[24 marks for content and organisation and 16 marks for technical accuracy; total 40 marks]

END OF QUESTIONS

English Language Paper 2: Writers' Viewpoints and Perspectives

- You are advised to spend about 15 minutes reading through the sources and all five questions.
- You should make sure you leave sufficient time to check your answers.

Section A: Reading

Answer all questions in this section.

You are advised to spend about 45 minutes on this section.

Source A is an extract from *Domestic Manners of the Americans*, by Frances Trollope, published in 1832. In this chapter the writer, an Englishwoman living in the USA, gives her reaction to what she sees as the 'familiarity' of Americans.

The extraordinary familiarity of our poor neighbours startled us at first, and we hardly knew how to receive their uncouth advances, or what was expected of us in return; however, it sometimes produced very laughable scenes. Upon one occasion two of my children set off upon an exploring walk up the hills; they were absent rather longer than we expected, and the rest of our party
5 determined upon going out to meet them; we knew the direction they had taken, but thought it would be as well to enquire at a little public-house at the bottom of the hill, if such a pair had been seen to pass. A woman, whose appearance more resembled a Covent Garden market-woman than any thing else I can remember, came out and answered my question with the most jovial good humour in the affirmative, and prepared to join us in our search. Her look, her voice, her
10 manner, were so exceedingly coarse and vehement, that she almost frightened me; she passed her arm within mine, and to the inexpressible amusement of my young people, she dragged me on, talking and questioning me without ceasing. She lived but a short distance from us, and I am sure intended to be a very good neighbour; but her violent intimacy made me dread to pass her door; my children, including my sons, she always addressed by their Christian names, excepting when
15 she substituted the word "honey;" this familiarity of address, however, I afterwards found was universal throughout all ranks in the United States.

My general appellation amongst my neighbours was "the English old woman," but in mentioning each other they constantly employed the term "lady;" and they evidently had a pleasure in using it, for I repeatedly observed, that in speaking of a neighbour, instead of saying Mrs. Such-a-one,
20 they described her as "the lady over the way what takes in washing," or as "that there lady, out by the Gulley, what is making dip-candles." Mr. Trollope was as constantly called "the old man," while draymen, butchers' boys, and the labourers on the canal were invariably denominated "them gentlemen;" nay, we once saw one of the most gentlemanlike men in Cincinnati introduce a fellow in dirty shirt sleeves, and all sorts of detestable et cetera, to one of his friends, with this formula,
25 "D – let me introduce this gentleman to you." Our respective titles certainly were not very important; but the eternal shaking hands with these ladies and gentlemen was really an annoyance, and the more so, as the near approach of the gentlemen was always redolent of whiskey and tobacco.

Source B is an article in which the writer expresses his opinion about customer service in restaurants.

CALL ME (SIR OR) MADAM

Sean Boyle wants to be served by a waiter, not a new best friend.

'Hey, guys! How are you doing?'

The first time I was greeted like this by a waiter in a (fairly upmarket)
5 restaurant, I was outraged. Obviously not a very classy joint, I thought, and
not one I would care to set foot in again. But it's got to the point now that if
I stuck to my guns and boycotted every establishment where I was spoken to
like a New York delinquent rather than a middle-aged British gentleman, I
would never leave the house.

10 And what is it about the word 'guys'? Suddenly, it's everywhere, applied to people of both genders and
all ages. It started with children's T.V. presenters, ever notorious for using Americanisms to 'get down with
the kids', and now it's everywhere. On television it's used to address not just hip young men from the streets
but elderly ladies buying antiques, minor celebrities learning to dance and even elected politicians. Go into
any school nowadays and you're likely to hear the appalling Americanism 'Listen up, guys' rather than, 'Pay
15 attention, children' or 'Be quiet, Class Four'. Whenever more than one person is addressed they are called
'you guys'. It's as if nobody is aware that the plural form of the pronoun 'you' is 'you'.

This kind of over-familiarity seems to have been imported from America – or copied from American
films and television. Yet – to bring us back to restaurants – friends who have lived in the USA tell me that
Americans are often more polite and formal than we are: being addressed as 'Sir' or 'Madam' is the norm.
20 Of course, you can get the forced friendliness of 'Hi, my name's Heidi. I'll be your server tonight.' That's
another irritating trend that's gaining a foothold over here – we don't need to know her name and we already
know what her job is. We're not here to get chummy with the staff; we just want them to bring us our food.
And when it happens in a British restaurant it just seems false. What we've imported is a stereotypical idea of
Stateside friendliness rather than genuine warmth and good manners.

25 I wonder if this need to embrace informality has something to do with a British dislike of servility. I used
to work in the service industry in London and – like most of my colleagues – was quite happy to address
customers as 'Sir' or 'Madam'. Yet I knew people who said they found this demeaning, as if by addressing
people in this way we were accepting that they were somehow superior to us.

It has been said this discomfort with the idea of serving others is a reaction to the time when huge numbers
30 of working class Britons spent their lives 'in service', often in 'Downton Abbey' style big houses, where
they were never allowed to forget their lowly status. Twenty-first century Britons bow to no-one. In contrast,
in countries like France and Italy, serving people is not considered demeaning. To serve is not to be servile.
Walk into almost any restaurant in these countries and you will greeted by 'Bonjour' or 'Buona Sera' and
addressed as 'Monsieur/Madame' or 'Signore/Signora'. In return you are expected to greet not only the staff
35 but the people sitting near you. When you've done that, you can get on with eating your meal, efficiently
served by a professional waiter – not by your new best friend, Luigi.

I don't want waiting staff and bar staff to touch their forelocks and grovel to me. But nor do I want my evening
out to turn into some kind of pseudo-American sitcom. There's a happy medium here, 'guys'. By all means be
friendly – there's nothing wrong with a cheerful smile as you say 'good evening' or even a brief chat about the
40 weather – but treat your customers with respect, starting with the use of 'Sir' and 'Madam'. And for the sake of
good customer relations, the English language and my blood pressure, please never, ever call us 'you guys'.

1. Read again the first paragraph of Source A (lines 1 to 16).

   Choose four statements below that are TRUE.
   • Shade the boxes of the ones that you think are true.
   • Choose a maximum of four statements.

   A. The neighbours are very unfriendly. ☐

   B. Frances Trollope has more than two children. ☐

   C. She knows which way the children went. ☐

   D. The woman says she has not seen the children. ☐

   E. The woman is quiet and gentle. ☐

   F. Trollope's children find the incident funny. ☐

   G. The neighbour calls Trollope's children by their first names. ☐

   H. The woman's familiarity is unusual in America. ☐

   [4 marks]

2. You need to refer to Source A and Source B for this question.

   Use details from both sources. Write a summary of the differences and similarities between the behaviour described by Trollope and by Boyle.   **[8 marks]**

3. You now need to refer only to Source A, the extract from *Domestic Manners of the Americans*.

   How does the writer use language to inform and entertain the reader?   **[12 marks]**

4. For this question, you need to refer to both Source A and Source B.

   Compare how the writers convey their attitudes to good manners and over-friendliness.

   In your answer you should:
   • compare their attitudes
   • compare the methods they use to convey these attitudes
   • support your ideas with quotations from both texts.   **[16 marks]**

Section B: Writing

You are advised to spend about 45 minutes on this section.

You are reminded of the need to plan your answer.

You should write in full sentences.

You should leave enough time to check your work at the end.

5. 'People claim now that they have hundreds or even thousands of friends – but they've never met most of them. In real life nobody has more than two or three true friends.'

Write an article for a magazine in which you explain your point of view on this statement.

[24 marks for content and organisation and 16 marks for technical accuracy; total 40 marks]

END OF QUESTIONS

English Literature Exam Papers

There are two English Literature Exams.

Paper 1 contains questions on Shakespeare and 19th Century Novels. In each section, you will answer one question on the text you have studied.

Paper 2 includes questions on Modern Prose or Drama and Poetry and Unseen Poetry. You will answer one question on the modern text you have studied (in the exam you will be given a choice between two questions on each text), a question on the section of the Poetry Anthology you have studied and a two-part question about two poems that you have not seen before.

All the texts that you might have studied are listed below:

Paper 1

Shakespeare

Macbeth

Romeo and Juliet

The Tempest

Much Ado About Nothing

The Merchant of Venice

Julius Caesar

The 19th Century Novel

The Strange Case of Doctor Jekyll and Mr Hyde by Robert Louis Stevenson

A Christmas Carol by Charles Dickens

Great Expectations by Charles Dickens

Jane Eyre by Charlotte Brontë

Frankenstein by Mary Shelley

Pride and Prejudice by Jane Austen

The Sign of Four by Sir Arthur Conan Doyle

Paper 2

Modern Prose or Drama

An Inspector Calls by JB Priestley

Blood Brothers by Willy Russell

The History Boys by Alan Bennett

DNA by Dennis Kelly

The Curious Incident of the Dog in the Night-Time by Simon Stephens

A Taste of Honey by Shelagh Delaney

Lord of the Flies by William Golding

Telling Tales (the AQA anthology of short stories)

Animal Farm by George Orwell

Never Let Me Go by Kazuo Ishiguro

Anita and Me by Meera Syal

Pigeon English by Stephen Kelman

Poetry

AQA Anthology: *Poems Past and Present*

Either 'Love and Relationships' **or** 'Power and Conflict'

Please note that line numbers given in the questions in the following pages may vary, according to which edition of the text you are using.

English Literature Practice Papers Set A

Pages 25–30: English Literature Paper 1: Shakespeare

The questions on pages 25–30 will help you to revise for:

- AQA Paper 1

Answer one question from this section on the play you have studied.

The marks for the questions are shown in square brackets.

Additional marks will be given for AO4 (spelling, punctuation and grammar)

Pages 31–37: English Literature Paper 1: The 19th Century Novel

The questions on pages 31–37 will help you to revise for:

- AQA Paper 1

Answer one question from this section on the novel you have studied.

The marks for the questions are shown in square brackets.

Pages 38–39: English Literature Paper 2: Modern Prose or Drama

The questions on pages 38–39 will help you to revise for:

- AQA Paper 2

Answer one question from this section on the text you have studied.

The marks for the questions are shown in square brackets.

Additional marks will be given for AO4 (spelling, punctuation and grammar)

Pages 40–43: English Literature Paper 2: Poetry and Unseen Poetry

The poetry questions on pages 40–41 will help you to revise for:

- AQA Paper 2

The unseen poetry questions on pages 42–43 will help you to revise for:

- AQA Paper 2

Name: ....

English Literature Paper 1: Shakespeare

Answer the question on the play you have studied.

You should spend about 50 minutes answering the question.

1. *Macbeth*

Read the following extract from Act 4 Scene 3 and then answer the question that follows.

At this point in the play, Malcolm has just told Macduff that his family has been killed on Macbeth's orders.

MALCOLM
                                  Be comforted.
Let's make us medicines of our great revenge
To cure this deadly grief.
MACDUFF
He has no children. All my pretty ones!
5 Did you say all? O hell-kite! All?
What, all my pretty chickens and their dam
At one fell swoop?
MALCOLM

Dispute it like a man.
MACDUFF

I shall do so,
10 But I must also feel it as a man.
I cannot but remember such things were
That were most precious to me. Did heaven look on
And would not take their part? Sinful Macduff,
They were all struck for thee. Naught that I am,
15 Not for their own demerits but for mine
Fell slaughter on their souls. Heaven rest them now,
MALCOLM

Be this the whetstone of your sword. Let grief
Convert to anger: blunt not the heart, enrage it.
MACDUFF

O, I could play the woman with mine eyes
20 And braggart with my tongue! But gentle heavens
Cut short all intermission. Front to front
Bring thou this fiend of Scotland and myself.
Within my sword's length set him. If he 'scape,
Heaven forgive him too.

Starting with this extract, explore how Shakespeare presents Macduff's character in *Macbeth*.

Write about:
- how Shakespeare presents Macduff in this extract
- how Shakespeare presents Macduff in the play as a whole.

[30 marks]
AO4 [4 marks]

2. *Romeo and Juliet*

Read the following extract from Act 2 Scene 3 and then answer the question that follows.

Here, Friar Laurence reacts to the news that Romeo has fallen in love with Juliet.

> **FRIAR LAURENCE**
> Holy Saint Francis, what a change is here!
> Is Rosaline, that thou didst love so dear,
> So soon forsaken? Young men's love then lies
> Not truly in their hearts, but in their eyes.
> 5 Jesu Maria, what a deal of brine
> Hath washed thy sallow cheek for Rosaline!
> How much salt water thrown away in waste
> To season love, that of it doth not taste!
> The sun not yet thy sighs from heaven clears.
> 10 Thy old groans yet ring in my ancient ears.
> Lo, here upon thy cheek the stain doth sit
> Of an old tear that is not washed off yet.
> If e'er thou wast thyself, and these woes thine,
> Thou and these woes were all for Rosaline.
> 15 And art thou changed? Pronounce this sentence then:
> Women may fall when there's no strength in men.
> **ROMEO**
> Thou chidd'st me oft for loving Rosaline
> **FRIAR LAURENCE**
> For doting, not for loving, pupil mine.
> **ROMEO**
> And bad'st me bury love.
> **FRIAR LAURENCE**
>   Not in a grave
> 20 To lay one in, another out to have.
> **ROMEO**
> I pray thee, chide me not. Her I love now
> Doth grace for grace and love for love allow.

Starting with this extract, explore how Shakespeare presents attitudes to love in *Romeo and Juliet*.

Write about:
- how Shakespeare presents attitudes to love in this extract
- how Shakespeare presents attitudes to love in the play as a whole.

[30 marks]
AO4 [4 marks]

3. **The Tempest**

Read the following extract from Act 2 Scene 2 and then answer the question that follows.

In this scene, Stefano and Trinculo have made Caliban drunk and he has sworn to serve Stefano instead of Prospero.

CALIBAN
I prithee, let me bring thee where crabs grow,
And I with my long nails will dig thee pig-nuts,
Show thee a jay's nest, and instruct thee how
To snare the nimble marmoset. I'll bring thee
5   To clust'ring filberts, and sometimes I'll get thee
Young seamews from the rock. Wilt thou go with me?
STEFANO
I prithee now, lead the way, without any more talking. Trinculo, the King and all our company
else being drowned, we will inherit here. Here, bear my bottle. Fellow Trinculo, we'll fill him
by and by again.
CALIBAN (*sings drunkenly*)
10   Farewell, master, farewell, farewell!
TRINCULO
A howling monster, a drunken monster!
CALIBAN (*sings*)
No more dams I'll make for fish.
Nor fetch in firing
At requiring,
15   Nor scrape trenchering, nor wash dish.
'Ban, 'ban, Cacaliban.
Has a new master. Get a new man!
Freedom, high-day! High-day, freedom! Freedom, high-day, freedom!

Starting with this extract, explain how Shakespeare writes about slavery and freedom in *The Tempest*.

Write about:
• how Shakespeare presents ideas about slavery and freedom in this extract
• how Shakespeare presents ideas about slavery and freedom in the play as a whole.   **[30 marks]**
AO4 [4 marks]

4. **Much Ado about Nothing**

Read the following extract from Act 1 Scene 3 and then answer the question that follows.

Here, Don John discusses his sad mood and discontent with Conrad.

DON JOHN

I cannot hide what I am. I must be sad when I have cause, and smile at no man's jests; eat when I have stomach, and wait for no man's leisure; sleep when I am drowsy, and tend on no man's business; laugh when I am merry, and claw no man in his humour.

CONRAD

Yea, but you must not make the full show of this till you may do it without controlment. You
5   of late stood out against your brother, and he hath ta'en you newly into his grace, where it is impossible you should take true root but by the fair weather that you make yourself. It is needful that you frame the season for your own harvest.

DON JOHN

I had rather be a canker in a hedge than a rose in his grace, and it better fits my blood to be disdained of all than to fashion a carriage to rob love from any. In this, though I cannot be
10 said to be a flattering honest man, it must not be denied but I am a plain-dealing villain. I am trusted with a muzzle, and enfranchised with a clog. Therefore I have decreed not to sing in my cage. If I had my mouth I would bite. If I had my liberty I would do my liking. In the mean time, let me be that I am, and seek not to alter me.

CONRAD

Can you make no use of your discontent?

Starting with this conversation, explore how Shakespeare presents the character of Don John as a villain in *Much Ado about Nothing*.

Write about:
• how Shakespeare presents Don John in this extract
• how Shakespeare presents Don John in the play as a whole.

[30 marks]
AO4 [4 marks]

5. **The Merchant of Venice**

Read the following extract from Act 3 Scene 2 and then answer the question that follows.

Here, Portia explains her feelings to Bassanio before he chooses a casket.

> **PORTIA**
> I pray you tarry. Pause a day or two
> Before you hazard, for in choosing wrong
> I lose your company; therefore forbear a while.
> There's something tells me, but it is not love,
> 5 I would not lose you; and you know yourself
> Hate counsels not in such a quality.
> But lest you should not understand me well –
> And yet a maiden hath no tongue but thought –
> I would detain you here some month or two
> 10 Before you venture for me. I could teach you
> How to choose right, but then I am forsworn.
> So will I never be. So may you miss me;
> But if you do, you'll make me wish a sin,
> That I had been forsworn. Beshrew your eyes!
> 15 They have o'erlooked me and divided me:
> One half of me is yours, the other half yours –
> And so all yours. O these naughty times
> Put bars between the owners and their rights!
> And so though yours, not yours. Prove it so.
> 20 Let Fortune go to hell for it, not I.

Starting with this speech, explore how Shakespeare presents the role of women in *The Merchant of Venice.*

Write about:
• how Shakespeare presents the role of women in this speech
• how Shakespeare presents the role of women in the play as a whole.   **[30 marks]**
      AO4 [4 marks]

6. *Julius Caesar*

Read the following extract from Act 5 Scene 5 and then answer the question that follows.

At this point in the play, after losing the final battle, Brutus has killed himself.

> **MESSALA**
> How died my master, Strato?
> **STRATO**
> I held his sword, and he did run upon it.
> **MESSALA**
> Octavius, then take him to follow thee,
> That did the latest service to my master.
> **ANTONY**
> 5   This was the noblest Roman of them all.
> All the conspirators save only he
> Did that they did in envy of great Caesar.
> He only in a general honest thought
> And common good to all made one of them.
> 10 His life was gentle, and the elements
> So mixed in that him nature might stand up
> And say to all the world 'This was a man'.
> **OCTAVIUS**
> According to his virtue let us use him,
> With all respect and rites of burial.
> 15 Within my tent his bones tonight shall lie,
> Most like a soldier, ordered honourably.
> So call the field to rest, and let's away
> To part the glories of this happy day.

Starting with this extract, explore how Shakespeare presents Brutus as 'the noblest Roman of them all' in *Julius Caesar.*

Write about:
- how Shakespeare presents Brutus in this extract
- how Shakespeare presents Brutus in the play as a whole.

[30 marks]
AO4 [4 marks]

English Literature Paper 1: The 19ᵗʰ Century Novel

Answer the question on the novel you have studied.

You should spend about 50 minutes answering the question.

1. **Robert Louis Stevenson:** *The Strange Case of Doctor Jekyll and Mr Hyde*

   Read the following extract from Chapter 10 and then answer the question that follows.

   In this extract, Jekyll describes how he first experimented on himself and turned into Mr Hyde.

I had long since prepared my tincture; I purchased at once, from a firm of wholesale chemists, a large quantity of a particular salt which I knew, from my experiments, to be the last ingredient required; and late one accursed night, I compounded the elements, watched them boil and smoke together in the glass, and when the ebullition had subsided, with a strong
5 glow of courage, drank off the potion.

The most racking pangs succeeded: a grinding in the bones, deadly nausea, and a horror of the spirit that cannot be exceeded at the hour of birth or death. Then these agonies began swiftly to subside, and I came to myself as if out of a great sickness. There was something strange in my sensations, something indescribably new from its very novelty, incredibly sweet. I
10 felt younger, lighter, happier in body; within I was conscious of a heady recklessness, a current of disordered sensual images running like a millrace in my fancy, a solution of the bonds of obligation, an unknown but not an innocent freedom of the soul. I knew myself, at the first breath of this new life, to be more wicked, tenfold more wicked, sold a slave to my original evil; and the thought, in that moment, braced and delighted me like wine. I stretched out my
15 hands, exulting in the freshness of these sensations; and in the act, I was suddenly aware that I had lost in stature.

There was no mirror, at that date, in my room; that which stands beside me as I write, was brought there later on and for the very purpose of these transformations. The night however, was far gone into the morning - the morning, black as it was, was nearly ripe for
20 the conception of the day - the inmates of my house were locked in the most rigorous hours of slumber; and I determined, flushed as I was with hope and triumph, to venture in my new shape as far as to my bedroom. I crossed the yard, wherein the constellations looked down upon me, I could have thought, with wonder, the first creature of that sort that their unsleeping vigilance had yet disclosed to them; I stole through the corridors, a stranger in my
25 own house; and coming to my room, I saw for the first time the appearance of Edward Hyde.

Starting with this extract, write about how Stevenson explores ideas about the possibilities and dangers of science in *The Strange Case of Doctor Jekyll and Mr Hyde.*

Write about:
- how Stevenson writes about Jekyll's actions in this extract
- how he uses the 'strange case' to explore ideas about the possibilities and dangers of science in the novel as a whole. **[30 marks]**

2. **Charles Dickens: *A Christmas Carol***

Read the following extract from Stave (Chapter) 2 and then answer the question that follows.

In this extract, the Ghost of Christmas Past appears to Scrooge and takes him on a journey into his past.

> 'Are you the Spirit, sir, whose coming was foretold to me?' asked Scrooge.
>
> 'I am!'
>
> The voice was soft and gentle. Singularly low, as if instead of being so close beside him, it were at a distance.
>
> 5   'Who, and what are you?' Scrooge demanded.
>
> 'I am the Ghost of Christmas Past.'
>
> 'Long past?' inquired Scrooge; observant of its dwarfish stature.
>
> 'No. Your past.'
>
> Perhaps Scrooge could not have told anybody why, if anybody could have asked him; but he
> 10   had a special desire to see the Spirit in his cap; and begged him to be covered.
>
> 'What!' exclaimed the Ghost, 'would you so soon put out, with worldly hands, the light I give? Is it not enough that you are one of those whose passions made this cap, and force me through whole trains of years to wear it low upon my brow?'
>
> Scrooge reverently disclaimed all intention to offend or any knowledge of having wilfully
> 15   bonneted the Spirit at any period of his life. He then made bold to inquire what business brought him there.
>
> 'Your welfare!' said the Ghost.
>
> Scrooge expressed himself much obliged, but could not help thinking that a night of unbroken rest would have been more conducive to that end. The Spirit must have heard him
> 20   thinking, for it said immediately: 'Your reclamation, then. Take heed!'
>
> It put out its strong hand as it spoke, and clasped him gently by the arm.
>
> 'Rise! and walk with me!'

Starting with this extract, explain how Dickens writes about how Scrooge has been shaped by his experiences.

Write about:

- how Dickens writes about Scrooge and the Ghost of Christmas Past in this extract
- how Dickens explores how Scrooge's experiences have shaped his character in the novel as a whole.

[30 marks]

3. **Charles Dickens: *Great Expectations***

Read the following extract from Chapter 18 and then answer the question that follows.

In this extract Pip, Joe and Biddy discuss Pip's plans for buying new clothes before he leaves for London.

At those times I would get up and look out at the door; for, our kitchen door opened at once upon the night, and stood open on summer evenings to air the room. The very stars to which I then raised my eyes, I am afraid I took to be but poor and humble stars for glittering on the rustic objects among which I had passed my life.

5 'Saturday night,' said I, when we sat at our supper of bread-and-cheese and beer. 'Five more days, and then the day before the day! They'll soon go.'

'Yes, Pip,' observed Joe, whose voice sounded hollow in his beer mug. 'They'll soon go.'

'Soon, soon go,' said Biddy.

10 'I have been thinking, Joe, that when I go down on Monday, and order my new clothes, I shall tell the tailor that I'll come and put them on there, or that I'll have them sent to Mr Pumblechook's. It would be very disagreeable to be stared at by all the people here.'

'Mr and Mrs Hubble might like to see you in your new gen-teel figure too, Pip,' said Joe, industriously cutting his bread, with his cheese on it, in the palm of his left hand, and glancing

15 at my untasted supper as if he thought of the time when we used to compare slices. 'So might Wopsle. And the Jolly Bargemen might take it as a compliment.'

'That's just what I don't want, Joe. They would make such a business of it – such a coarse and common business – that I couldn't bear it myself.'

Ah, that indeed, Pip!' said Joe. 'If you couldn't abear your- self –'

20 Biddy asked me here, as she sat holding my sister's plate, 'Have you thought about when you'll show yourself to Mr Gargery, and your sister, and me? You will show yourself to us; won't you?'

Biddy,' I returned with some resentment, 'you are so exceedingly quick that it's difficult to keep up with you.'

25 ('She always were quick,' observed Joe.)

'If you had waited another moment, Biddy, you would have heard me say that I shall bring my clothes here in a bundle one evening – most likely on the evening before I go away.'

Biddy said no more. Handsomely forgiving her, I soon exchanged an affectionate good-night with her and Joe, and went up to bed.

Starting with this extract, write about how Dickens uses Pip to explore ideas about social class.

Write about:
- how Dickens writes about differences in social class and Pip's attitudes to them in this extract
- how Dickens uses Pip to explore social class and attitudes to it in the novel as a whole. **[30 marks]**

4. Charlotte Brontë: *Jane Eyre*

Read the following extract from Chapter 26 and then answer the question that follows.

In this extract, Jane and Rochester are about to be married when the ceremony is interrupted.

> We entered the quiet and humble temple; the priest waited in his white surplice at the lowly altar, the clerk beside him. All was still: two shadows only moved in a remote corner. My conjecture had been correct: the strangers had slipped in before us, and they now stood by the vault of the Rochesters, their backs towards us, viewing through the rails the old-time stained
> 5   marble tomb, where a kneeling angel guarded the remains of Damer de Rochester, slain at Marston Moor, in the time of the civil wars, and of Elizabeth, his wife.
>
> Our place was taken at the communion rails. Hearing a cautious step behind me, I glanced over my shoulder: one of the strangers – a gentleman, evidently – was advancing up the chapel. The service began. The explanation of the intent of matrimony was gone through; and
> 10   then the clergyman came a step further forward, and, bending slightly towards Mr Rochester, went on:
>
> 'I require and charge you both (as ye will answer at the dreadful Day of Judgement when the secrets of all hearts shall be disclosed), that if either of you know of any impediment why ye may not lawfully be joined together in matrimony, ye do now confess it; for be ye well
> 15   assured that so many as are coupled together otherwise than God's Word doth allow, are not joined together by God, neither is their matrimony lawful.'
>
> He paused, as the custom is. When is the pause after that sentence ever broken by reply? Not perhaps, once in a hundred years. And the clergyman, who had not lifted his eyes from the book, and had held his breath but for a moment, was proceeding: his hand was already
> 20   stretched towards Mr Rochester, as his lips unclosed to ask, 'Wilt thou have this woman for thy wedded wife?' – when a distinct and near voice said –
>
> 'The marriage cannot go on: I declare the existence of an impediment.'

Starting with this extract, write about how Brontë presents faith and religion, and their importance to Jane.

Write about:

- how Brontë writes about Jane's feelings about the church and the wedding ceremony in this extract
- how Brontë writes about faith and religion in the novel as a whole. **[30 marks]**

5. Mary Shelley: *Frankenstein*

Read the following extract from Chapter 10 and then answer the question that follows.

In this extract, Victor Frankenstein seeks comfort in nature as he climbs Mount Montanvert.

> The ascent is precipitous, but the path is cut into continual and short windings, which enable you to surmount the perpendicularity of the mountain. It is a scene terrifically desolate. In a thousand spots the traces of the winter avalanche may be perceived, where trees lie broken and strewed on the ground, some entirely destroyed, others bent, leaning upon the jutting
> 5 rocks of the mountain or transversely upon other trees. The path, as you ascend higher, is intersected by ravines of snow, down which stones continually roll from above; one of them is particularly dangerous, as the slightest sound, such as even speaking in a loud voice, produces a concussion of air sufficient to draw destruction upon the head of the speaker. The pines are not tall or luxuriant, but they are sombre and add an air of severity to the scene. I looked on
> 10 the valley beneath; vast mists were rising from the rivers which ran through it and curling in thick wreaths around the opposite mountains, whose summits were hid in the uniform clouds, while rain poured from the dark sky and added to the melancholy impression I received from the objects around me, Alas! Why does man boast of sensibilities superior to those apparent in the brute; it only renders them more necessary beings. If our impulses were confined to
> 15 hunger, thirst and desire, we might be nearly free; but now we are moved by every wind that blows and a chance word or scene that that word may convey to us.

Starting with this extract, write about how Shelley writes about nature in *Frankenstein*.

Write about:

- how Shelley writes about nature in this extract
- how Shelley explores nature and attitudes to nature in the novel as a whole. **[30 marks]**

6. **Jane Austen: *Pride and Prejudice***

Read the following extract from Chapter 23 and then answer the question that follows.

In this extract, Mr and Mrs Bennet react to the news that Charlotte Lucas is to be married to Mr Collins.

Mrs Bennet was in fact too much overpowered to say a great deal while Sir William remained; but no sooner had he left them than her feelings found a rapid vent. In the first place, she persisted in disbelieving the whole of the matter; secondly, she was very sure that Mr Collins had been taken in; thirdly, she trusted that they would never be happy together; and
5 fourthly, that the match would be broken off. Two inferences, however, were plainly deduced from the whole; one, that Elizabeth was the real cause of all the mischief; and the other, that she herself had been barbarously used by them all; and on these two points she principally dwelt during the rest of the day. Nothing could console and nothing could appease her. Nor did that day wear out her resentment. A week elapsed before she could see Elizabeth without
10 scolding her, a month passed away before she could speak to Sir William or Lady Lucas without being rude, and many months were gone before she could at all forgive their daughter.

Mr Bennet's emotions were much more tranquil on the occasion, and such as he did experience he pronounced to be of a most agreeable sort; for it gratified him, he said, to discover that Charlotte Lucas, whom he had used to think tolerably sensible, was as foolish as
15 his wife, and more foolish than his daughter!

Starting with this extract, explore how Austen writes about the Bennets as parents in *Pride and Prejudice*.

Write about:

*   how Austen writes about Mr and Mrs Bennet as parents in this extract
*   how Austen writes about Mr and Mrs Bennet as parents in the novel as a whole. **[30 marks]**

7. **Sir Arthur Conan Doyle: *The Sign of Four***

Read the following extract from Chapter 1 and then answer the question that follows.

In this extract, Holmes and Watson discuss Holmes's career and Watson's account of one of his cases.

'The only official consulting detective,' he answered. 'I am the last and highest court of appeal in detection. When Gregson or Lestrade or Athelney Jones are out of their depths – which, by the way, is their normal state – the matter is laid before me. I examine the data, as an expert, and pronounce a specialist's opinion. I claim no credit in such cases. My name figures
5 in no newspaper. The work itself, the pleasure of finding a field for my peculiar powers, is my highest reward. But you yourself had some experience of my methods of work in the Jefferson Hope case.'

'Yes, indeed,' said I, cordially. 'I was never so struck by anything in my life. I even embodied in a small brochure with the somewhat fantastic title of 'A Study in Scarlet'.'

10 He shook his head sadly. 'I glanced over it,' said he. 'Honestly, I cannot congratulate you upon it. Detection is, or ought to be, an exact science, and should be treated in the same cold and unemotional manner. You have attempted to tinge it with romanticism, which produces much the same effect as if you worked a love-story or an elopement into the fifth proposition of Euclid.'

15 'But the romance was there,' I remonstrated. 'I could not tamper with the facts.'

'Some facts should be suppressed, or at least a just sense of proportion should be observed in treating them. The only point in the case which deserved mention was the curious analytical reasoning from effects to causes by which I succeeded in unravelling it.'

I was annoyed at this criticism of a work which had been specially designed to please him.
20 I confess, too, that I was irritated by the egotism which seemed to demand that every line of my pamphlet should be devoted to his own special doings. More than once during the years that I had lived with him in Baker Street I had observed that a small vanity underlay my companion's quiet and didactic manner. I made no remark, however, but sat nursing my wounded leg. I had a Jezail bullet through it some time before, and though it did not prevent
25 me from walking, it ached wearily at every change of the weather.

Starting with this extract, explore how Conan Doyle uses Watson as a narrator in *The Sign of Four*.

Write about:
*   how Conan Doyle uses Watson as a narrator in this extract
*   how Conan Doyle uses Watson as a narrator in the novel as a whole. **[30 marks]**

English Literature Paper 2: Modern Prose or Drama

Section A

Answer one question on the text you have studied.

You should spend between 45 and 50 minutes on the question.

N.B. In the exam you will be given a choice of two questions to choose from.

1. **J. B. Priestley: *An Inspector Calls***

   How does Priestley write about social problems in *An Inspector Calls*?

   Write about:
   * the social problems that Priestley writes about in *An Inspector Calls*
   * how Priestley presents these problems by the way he writes.

   [30 marks]
   AO4 [4 marks]

2. **Willy Russell: *Blood Brothers***

   Do Mickey and his mother create their own tragedy in *Blood Brothers* or are they just victims?

   Write about:
   * what Mickey and Mrs Johnstone do and what happens to them
   * how Russell writes about what they do and what happens to them.

   [30 marks]
   AO4 [4 marks]

3. **Alan Bennett: *The History Boys***

   How does Bennett use the Headmaster to present ideas about education and authority in *The History Boys*?

   Write about:
   * what the Headmaster does and says
   * how Bennett presents the Headmaster in the play.

   [30 marks]
   AO4 [4 marks]

4. **Dennis Kelly: *DNA***

   How does Kelly write about the way teenagers can behave in *DNA*?

   Write about:
   * the actions taken by the teenage characters in *DNA*
   * how Kelly presents their actions in the play.

   [30 marks]
   AO4 [4 marks]

5. **Simon Stephens: *The Curious Incident of the Dog in the Night-Time***

   How does Stephens present the character Christopher as being different from other people in *The Curious Incident of the Dog in the Night-Time*?

   Write about:
   * things Christopher does and says that indicate his 'difference'
   * how Stephens presents Christopher as being different from other characters.

   [30 marks]
   AO4 [4 marks]

6. **Shelagh Delaney: *A Taste of Honey***

How does Delaney write about women's attitudes towards men in *A Taste of Honey*?

Write about:
- how Delaney presents male characters and what they say and do
- how Helen and Jo react to and talk about men.

[30 marks]
AO4 [4 marks]

7. **William Golding: *Lord of the Flies***

Is Simon an important character in *Lord of the Flies*?

Write about:
- how Golding presents the character of Simon
- the significance of Simon in *Lord of the Flies*.

[30 marks]
AO4 [4 marks]

8. **AQA Anthology: *Telling Tales***

How do writers explore relationships between people of different generations in 'Korea' and one other story from *Telling Tales*?

Write about:
- the relationships described in the two stories
- how the writers present these relationships.

[30 marks]
AO4 [4 marks]

9. **George Orwell: *Animal Farm***

How does Orwell use old Major and his dream to write about idealism?

Write about:
- how Orwell presents old Major's ideals
- how Orwell uses old Major's ideals to explore the results and limits of idealism.

[30 marks]
AO4 [4 marks]

10. **Kazuo Ishiguro: *Never Let Me Go***

How does Ishiguro present Kathy and what difference does her role as narrator make to our reading of *Never Let Me Go*?

Write about:
- how Ishiguro presents Kathy's character in *Never Let Me Go*
- how she uses language as the narrator of *Never Let Me Go*.

[30 marks]
AO4 [4 marks]

11. **Meera Syal: *Anita and Me***

How does Syal present Indian culture and tradition in *Anita and Me*?

Write about:
- examples of Indian culture and traditions in *Anita and Me*
- how Syal writes about Indian culture and traditions.

[30 marks]
AO4 [4 marks]

12. **Stephen Kelman: *Pigeon English***

How does Kelman present violence and danger in *Pigeon English*?

Write about:
- examples of violent and dangerous behaviour in *Pigeon English*
- how Kelman presents violent and dangerous behaviour.

[30 marks]
AO4 [4 marks]

English Literature Paper 2: Poetry and Unseen Poetry

Section B: Poetry

AQA Anthology: *Poems Past and Present*

You should spend between 40 and 45 minutes on this question.

EITHER

---

1. Compare the way poets present ideas about memories in 'Eden Rock' and one other poem from 'Love and Relationships'. **[30 marks]**

> **Eden Rock**
>
> They are waiting for me somewhere beyond Eden Rock
> My father, twenty-five, in the same suit
> Of Genuine Irish Tweed, his terrier Jack
> Still two years old and trembling at his feet.
>
> My mother, twenty-three, in a sprigged dress
> Drawn at the waist, ribbon on her straw hat.
> Has spread the stiff white cloth over the grass.
> Her hair, the colour of wheat, takes on the light.
>
> She pours from a Thermos, the milk straight
> From an old H.P. sauce bottle, a screw
> Of paper for a cork; slowly sets out
> The same three plates, the tin cups painted in blue.
>
> The sky whitens as if lit by three suns.
> My mother shades her eyes and looks my way
> Over the drifted stream. My father spins
> A stone along the water. Leisurely,
>
> They beckon to me from the other bank.
> I hear them call, 'See where the stream-path is!
> Crossing is not as hard as you think.'
>
> I had not thought that it would be like this.
>
> **Charles Causley**
>
> Somebody asked me the other day where Eden Rock is – I mean, I have no idea,
> I made it up! 'Dartmoor,' I said - that's always a safe answer.

2. Compare the way poets write about war in 'Bayonet Charge' and one other poem from 'Power and Conflict'.

[30 marks]

Bayonet Charge

Suddenly he was awake and running – raw

In raw-seamed hot khaki, his sweat heavy,

Stumbling across a field of clods towards a green hedge

That dazzled with rifle fire, hearing

Bullets smacking the belly out of the air –

He lugged a rifle numb as a smashed arm;

The patriotic tear that had brimmed in his eye

Sweating like molten iron from the centre of his chest, -

In bewilderment then he almost stopped –

In what cold clockwork of the stars and the nations

Was he the hand pointing that second? He was running

Like a man who has jumped up in the dark and runs

Listening between his footfalls for the reason

Of his still running, and his foot hung like

Statuary in mid-stride. Then the shot-slashed furrows

Threw up a yellow hare that rolled like a flame

And crawled in a threshing circle, its mouth wide

Open silent, its eyes standing out.

He plunged past with his bayonet toward the green hedge,

King, honour, human dignity, etcetera

Dropped like luxuries in a yelling alarm

To get out of that blue crackling air

His terror's touchy dynamite.

Ted Hughes

Section C: Unseen Poetry

Answer both questions in this section.

You should spend a total of between 45 and 50 minutes on both questions.

Past and Present

I remember, I remember
The house where I was born,
The little window where the sun
Came peeping in at morn;
He never came a wink too soon
Nor brought too long a day;
But now, I often wish the night
Had borne my breath away.

I remember, I remember
The roses, red and white,
The violets and the lily-cups-
Those flowers made of light!
The lilacs where the robin built,
And where my brother set
The laburnum on his birthday,-
The tree is living yet!

I remember, I remember
Where I was used to swing,
And thought the air must rush as fresh
To swallows on the wing;
My spirit flew in feathers then
That is so heavy now,
And summer pools could hardly cool
The fever on my brow.

I remember, I remember
The fir trees dark and high;
I used to think their slender tops
Were close against the sky:
It was a childish ignorance,
But now 'tis little joy
To know I'm farther off from Heaven
Than when I was a boy.

Thomas Hood

1. In 'Past and Present' how does the poet present his feelings about his childhood? **[24 marks]**

> **The Swing**
>
> How do you like to go up in a swing,
> Up in the air so blue?
> Oh, I do think it the pleasantest thing
> Ever a child can do!
>
> Up in the air and over the wall,
> Till I can see so wide,
> River and trees and cattle and all
> Over the countryside–
>
> Till I look down on the garden green,
> Down on the roof so brown–
> Up in the air I go flying again,
> Up in the air and down!
>
> **Robert Louis Stevenson**

2. In both 'Past and Present' and 'The Swing' the poets write about children.
   What are the similarities and/or differences between the ways the poets present
   their feelings? **[8 marks]**

END OF QUESTIONS

English Literature Practice Papers Set B

Pages 45–50: English Literature Paper 1: Shakespeare

The questions on pages 45–50 will help you to revise for:

- AQA Paper 1

Answer one question from this section on the play you have studied.

The marks for the questions are shown in square brackets.

Additional marks will be given for AO4 (spelling, punctuation and grammar)

Pages 51–57: English Literature Paper 1: The 19th Century Novel

The questions on pages 51–57 will help you to revise for:

- AQA Paper 1

Answer one question from this section on the novel you have studied.

The marks for the questions are shown in square brackets.

Pages 58–61: English Literature Paper 2: Modern Prose or Drama

The questions on pages 58–61 will help you to revise for:

- AQA Paper 2

Answer one question from this section on the text you have studied.

The marks for the questions are shown in square brackets.

Additional marks will be given for AO4 (spelling, punctuation and grammar)

Pages 62–65: English Literature Paper 2: Poetry and Unseen Poetry

The poetry questions on pages 62–63 will help you to revise for:

- AQA Paper 2

The unseen poetry questions on pages 64–65 will help you to revise for:

- AQA Paper 2

The marks for the questions are shown in square brackets.

Name: ....

English Literature Paper 1: Shakespeare

Answer the question on the play you have studied.
You should spend about 50 minutes answering the question.

1. *Macbeth*

   Read the following extract from Act 3 Scene 4 and then answer the question that follows.

   At this point in the play, Macbeth has just seen Banquo's ghost.

MACBETH

It will have blood, they say. Blood will have blood.

Stones have been known to move and trees to speak,

Augurs and understood relations have

By maggot-pies and choughs and rooks brought forth

5 The secret'st man of blood. What is the night?

LADY MACBETH

Almost at odds with morning, which is which.

MACBETH

How sayst thou that Macduff denies his person

At our great bidding?

LADY MACBETH

            Did you send to him, sir?

MACBETH

I hear it by the way, but I will send.

10 There's not a one of them but in his house

I keep a servant fee'd. I will tomorrow,

And betimes I will, to the weird sisters.

More shall they speak, for now I am bent to know

By the worst means the worst. For mine own good

15 All causes shall give way. I am in blood

Steeped in so far that, should I wade no more,

Returning were as tedious as go o'er.

Strange things I have in head that will to hand,

Which must be acted ere they may be scanned

LADY MACBETH

20 You lack the season of all natures, sleep.

MACBETH

Come, we'll to sleep. My strange and self-abuse

Is the initiate fear that wants hard use.

We are yet but young in deed.

Starting with this extract, explore how Shakespeare shows Macbeth becoming more ruthless and tyrannical during the course of the play.

Write about:

* how Shakespeare presents Macbeth becoming ruthless and tyrannical in this extract
* how Shakespeare presents Macbeth becoming ruthless and tyrannical in the play as a whole.

[30 marks] AO4 [4 marks]

2. Romeo and Juliet

Read the following extract from Act 4 Scene 3 and then answer the question that follows.

In this extract, Juliet takes the poison that she has been given by Friar Laurence.

> **JULIET**
> How if, when I am laid into the tomb,
> I wake before the time that Romeo
> Come to redeem me? There's a fearful point.
> Shall I not then be stifled in the vault,
> 5 To whose foul mouth no healthsome air breathes in,
> And there die strangled ere my Romeo comes?
> Or, if I live, is it not very like
> The horrible conceit of death and night,
> Together with the terror of the place –
> 10 As in a vault, an ancient receptacle
> Where for this many hundred years the bones
> Of all my buried ancestors are packed;
> Where bloody Tybalt, yet but green in earth,
> Lies festering in his shroud; where, as they say,
> 15 At some hours in the night spirits resort –
> Alack, alack, is it not like that I,
> So early waking – what with loathsome smells,
> And shrieks like mandrakes torn out of the earth,
> That living mortals, hearing them, run mad –
> 20 Oh. If I wake, shall I not be distraught,
> Environed with all these hideous fears,
> And madly play with my forefathers' joints,
> And pluck the mangled Tybalt from his shroud,
> And, in this rage, with some great kinsman's bone
> 25 As with a club dash out my desp'rate brains?
> O, look! Methinks I see my cousin's ghost
> Seeking out Romeo that did spit his body
> Upon a rapier's point. Stat, Tybalt, stay!
> Romeo. Romeo, Romeo! Here's drink. I drink to thee.

Starting with this speech, explore how Shakespeare presents the link between love and death in *Romeo and Juliet.*

Write about:
- how Shakespeare presents Juliet's feelings about love and death in this extract
- how Shakespeare presents links between love and death in the play as a whole.
[30 marks]
AO4 [4 marks]

3. **The Tempest**

Read the following extract from Act 3 Scene 1 and then answer the question that follows.

In this scene, Ferdinand and Miranda talk about their feelings for each other.

FERDINAND
    Admired Miranda!
Indeed the top of admiration, worth
What's dearest to the world. Full many a lady
I have eyed with best regard, and many a time
5 Th'harmony of their tongues hath into bondage
Brought my too diligent ear. For several virtues
Have I liked several women; never any
With so full soul but some defect in her
Did quarrel with the noblest grace she owed
10 And put it to the foil. But you, O you,
So perfect and so peerless are created
Of every creature's best.
MIRANDA
            I do not know
One of my sex, no woman's face remember
Save from my glass mine own; nor have I seen
15 More that I may call men than you, good friend,
And my dear father. How features are abroad
I am skilless of; but by my modesty.
The jewel in my dower, I would not wish
Any companion in the world but you;
20 Nor can imagination form a shape
Besides yourself to like of. But I prattle
Something too wildly, and my father's precepts
I therein do forget.

Starting with this conversation, explain how Shakespeare writes about love in *The Tempest*.

Write about:
• how Shakespeare presents Ferdinand and Miranda's love in this extract
• how Shakespeare presents love and ideas about love in the play as a whole.   **[30 marks]**
                                                                                       AO4 [4 marks]

4. **Much Ado about Nothing**

Read the following extract from Act 3 Scene 1 and then answer the question that follows.

Here, Hero and Ursula are playing a trick on Beatrice, talking about Benedick's feelings when they know she is listening.

> **HERO**
> He is the only man in Italy.
> Always excepted my dear Claudio.
> **URSULA**
> I pray you not be angry with me, madam,
> Speaking my fancy. Signor Benedick
> 5 For shape, for bearing, argument, and valour
> Goes foremost in report throughout Italy.
> **HERO**
> Indeed, he hath an excellent good name.
> **URSULA**
> His excellence did earn it ere he had it.
> When are you married. Madam?
> **HERO**
> 10 Why, everyday, tomorrow. Come, go in.
> I'll show thee some attires and have thy counsel
> Which is the best to furnish me tomorrow.
> **URSULA** *(aside)*
> She's limed, I warrant you. We have caught her, madam.
> **HERO** *(aside)*
> If it prove so, then loving goes by haps.
> 15 Some Cupid kills with arrows, some with traps.
> > *Exeunt Hero and Ursula*
> **BEATRICE**
> What fire is in mine ears? Can this be true?
> Stand I condemned for pride and scorn so much?
> Contempt, farewell; and maiden pride, adieu.
> No glory lives behind the back of such.
> 20 And, Benedick, love on. I will requite thee,
> Taming my wild heart to thy loving hand.
> If thou dost love, my kindness shall incite thee
> To bind our loves up in a holy band.
> For others say thou dost deserve, and I
> 25 Believe it better than reportingly.

Starting with this extract, explore how Shakespeare presents the theme of trickery and deception in *Much Ado about Nothing*.

Write about:
- how Shakespeare presents trickery and deception in this extract
- how Shakespeare presents trickery and deception in the play as a whole.

[30 marks]

AO4 [4 marks]

5. *The Merchant of Venice*

Read the following extract from Act 2 Scene 5 and then answer the question that follows.

Here, Shylock advises Jessica to lock herself away during the masque, not knowing that she has plans to elope with a Christian.

SHYLOCK

What, are there masques? Hear you me, Jessica.

Lock up my doors, and when you hear the drum

And the vile squealing of the wry-necked fife,

Clamber not you up to the casements then

5 Nor thrust your head into the public street

To gaze on Christian fools with varnished faces;

But stop my house's ears – I mean my casements –

Let not the sound of shallow foppery enter

My sober house. By Jacob's staff I swear

10 I have no mind of feasting forth tonight:

But I will go. Go you before me, sirrah;

Say I will come.

LANCELOT

        I will go before, sir. (*aside to Jessica*)

Mistress, look out at window for all this.

    There will come a Christian by

15   Will be worthy a Jewess' eye.

SHYLOCK

What says this fool of Hagar's offspring, ha?

JESSICA

His words were 'Farewell, mistress', nothing else.

SHYLOCK

The patch is kind enough, but a huge feeder,

Snail-slow in profit, and he sleeps by day

20 More than the wildcat. Drones hive not with me,

Therefore I part with him, and part with him

To one that I would have him help to waste

His borrowed purse. Well, Jessica, go in;

Perhaps I will return immediately.

25 Do as I bid you, shut doors after you.

Fast bind, fast find.

A proverb never stale in thrifty mind.

JESSICA

Farewell, and if my fortune be not crossed,

I have a father, you a daughter, lost.

Starting with this extract, explore how far Shylock is a sympathetic character in *The Merchant of Venice.*

Write about:

- how Shakespeare writes about Shylock in this extract
- how Shakespeare writes about Shylock in the play as a whole.

[30 marks]

AO4 [4 marks]

6. *Julius Caesar*

Read the following extract from Act 2 Scene 5 and then answer the question that follows.

Here, Brutus and Cassius are arguing about Brutus's punishment of one of their followers for taking bribes.

CASSIUS
That you have wronged me doth appear in this:
You have condemned and noted Lucius Pella
For taking bribes here of the Sardians,
Wherein my letters praying on his side,
5   I knew the man, was slighted off.
BRUTUS
You wronged yourself to write in such a cause.
CASSIUS
In such a time as this it is not meet
That every nice offence should bear his comment.
BRUTUS
Let me tell you, Cassius, you yourself
10   Are much condemned to have an itching palm,
To sell and mart your offices for gold
To undeservers.
CASSIUS
                    I, an itching palm?
You now that you are Brutus that speaks this,
Or, by the gods, this speech were else your last.
BRUTUS
15   The name of Cassius honours this corruption
And chastisement doth therefore hide his head.
CASSIUS
Chastisement?
BRUTUS
Remember March, the Ides of March, remember.
Did not great Julius bleed for justice' sake?
20   What villain touched his body, that did stab.
And not for justice? What, shall one of us,
That struck the foremost man of all this world
But for supporting robbers, shall we now
Contaminate our fingers with base bribes,
25   And sell the mighty space of our large honours
For so much trash as may be grasped thus?
I had rather be a dog and bay the moon
Than such a Roman.

Starting with this extract, explore how Shakespeare presents the relationship between Cassius and Brutus in *Julius Caesar*.

Write about:
- how Shakespeare writes about Cassius and Brutus in this extract
- how Shakespeare writes about their relationship in the play as a whole.   **[30 marks] AO4 [4 marks]**

English Literature Paper 1: The 19th Century Novel

Answer the question on the novel you have studied.

You should spend about 50 minutes answering the question.

1. **Robert Louis Stevenson:** *The Strange Case of Doctor Jekyll and Mr Hyde*

   Read the following extract from Chapter 7 and then answer the question that follows.

   In this extract, Mr Utterson and Mr Enfield see Dr Jekyll at his window.

   > The court was very cool and a little damp. And full of premature twilight, although the sky, high up overhead, was still bright with sunset. The middle one of the three windows was half way open; and sitting close beside it, taking the air with an infinite sadness of mien, like some disconsolate prisoner, Utterson saw Dr Jekyll.
   >
   > 5   'What! Jekyll!' he cried. 'I trust you are better.'
   >
   > 'I am very low, Utterson,' replied the doctor drearily, 'very low. It will not last long, thank God.'
   >
   > 'You stay too much indoors,' said the lawyer. 'You should be out, whipping up the circulation, like Mr Enfield and me. (This is my cousin – Mr Enfield – Dr Jekyll.) Come now; get
   >
   > 10   your hat and take a quick turn with us.'
   >
   > 'You are very good,' sighed the other. 'I should like to very much; but no, no, no, it is quite impossible; I dare not, But indeed, Utterson, I am very glad to see you; this is really a great pleasure; I would ask you and Mr Enfield up, but the place is really not fit.'
   >
   > 'Why then,' said the lawyer, good-naturedly, 'the best thing we can do is to stay down
   >
   > 15   here and speak to you from where we are.'
   >
   > 'That is just what I was about to venture to propose,' returned the doctor with a smile. But the words were hardly uttered, before the smile was struck out of his face and succeeded by an expression of such abject terror and despair, as froze the very blood of the two gentlemen below. They saw it but for a glimpse, for the window was instantly thrust down;
   >
   > 20   but that glance had been sufficient, and they turned and left the court without a word.

   Starting with this extract, write about how sympathetically Stevenson presents the character of Dr Jekyll in *The Strange Case of Doctor Jekyll and Mr Hyde*.

   Write about:
   - how Stevenson writes about Jekyll and how others react to him in this extract
   - how he writes about Jekyll in the novel as a whole.

   [30 marks]

2. Charles Dickens: *A Christmas Carol*

Read the following extract from Stave (Chapter) 4 and then answer the question that follows.

In this extract, Scrooge is watching the Cratchits after the 'death' of Tiny Tim.

> She hurried out to meet him; and little Bob in his comforter – he had need of it poor
> fellow – came in. His tea was ready for him on the hob, and they all tried who should help him
> to it most. Then the two young Cratchits got upon his knees, and laid, each child, a little cheek
> against his face, as if they said, 'Don't mind it, father. Don't be grieved!'
> 5   Bob was very cheerful with them, and spoke pleasantly to all the family. He looked at the
> work upon the table, and praised the industry and speed of Mrs Cratchit and the girls. They
> would be done long before Sunday, he said.
>   'Sunday! You went today, then, Robert?' said his wife.
>   'Yes, my dear,' returned Bob. 'I wish you could have gone. It would have done you good
> 10 to see how green a place it is. But you'll see it often. I promised him that I would walk there
> on a Sunday. My little, little child!' cried Bob. 'My little child!'
>   He broke down all at once. He couldn't help it. If he could have helped it, he and his child
> would have been farther apart, perhaps, than they were.
>   He left the room, and went upstairs into the room above, which was lighted cheerfully,
> 15 and hung with Christmas. There was a chair set close beside the child, and there were signs of
> someone having been there lately. Poor Bob sat down in it, and, when he had thought a little
> and composed himself, he kissed the little face. He was reconciled to what had happened, and
> went down again quite happy.
>   They drew about the fire, and talked; the girls and mother working still. Bob told them of
> 20 the extraordinary kindness of Mr Scrooge's nephew, whom he had scarcely seen but once, and
> who, meeting him in the street that day, and seeing that he looked a little – 'just a little down,
> you know,' said Bob, inquired what had happened to distress him. 'On which,' said Bob, 'for he
> is the pleasantest-spoken gentleman you ever heard, I told him. "I am heartily sorry for you,
> Mr Cratchit." He said, "and heartily sorry for your good wife." By-the-bye, how he ever knew
> 25 that I don't know.'

Starting with this extract, explore how Dickens writes about the Cratchit family and their importance in the novel.

Write about:
- how Dickens writes about the Cratchits in this extract
- how Dickens writes about the Cratchits in the novel as a whole. **[30 marks]**

3. **Charles Dickens: *Great Expectations***

Read the following extract from Chapter 1 and then answer the question that follows.

In this extract, Pip meets Magwitch for the first time.

> 'Hold your noise!' cried a terrible voice, as a man started up from among the graves at the side of the church porch. 'Keep still, you little devil, or I'll cut your throat!'
>
> A fearful man, all in coarse gray, with a great iron on his leg. A man with no hat, and with broken shoes, and with an old rag tied round his head. A man who had been soaked in water,
> 5   and smothered in mud, and lamed by stones, and cut by flints, and stung by nettles, and torn by briars; who limped, and shivered, and glared and growled; and whose teeth chattered in his head as he seized me by the chin.
>
> 'Oh! Don't cut my throat, sir,' I pleaded in terror. 'Pray, don't do it, sir.'
>
> 'Tell us your name!' said the man. 'Quick!'
>
> 10   'Pip, sir.'
>
> 'Once more,' said the man, staring at me, 'Give it mouth!'
>
> 'Pip. Pip, sir.'
>
> 'Show us where you live,' said the man. 'Pint out the place!'
>
> I pointed to where our village lay, on the flat inshore among the alder-trees and pollards,
> 15   a mile or more from the church.
>
> The man, after looking at me for a moment, turned me upside-down, and emptied my pockets. There was nothing in them but a piece of bread. When the church came to itself – for he was so sudden and strong that he made it go head over heels before me, and I saw the steeple under my feet – when the church came to itself, I say, I was seated on a high
> 20   tombstone, trembling, while he ate the bread ravenously.
>
> 'You young dog,' said the man, licking his lips, 'what fat cheeks you ha' got.'
>
> I believe they were fat, though I was at that time undersized for my years, and not strong.
>
> 'Darn me if I couldn't eat 'em,' said the man, with a threatening shake of his head, 'and if I han't half a mind to't!'

Starting with this extract, write about how Dickens presents the character of Magwitch and his relationship with Pip.

Write about:
- how Dickens writes about Magwitch and the impression he makes on Pip in this extract
- how Dickens writes about Magwitch and his relationship with Pip in the novel as a whole.

[30 marks]

4. Charlotte Brontë: *Jane Eyre*

Read the following extract from Chapter 17 and then answer the question that follows.

In this extract, Jane leaves the room where Mr Rochester is entertaining his friends.

> I then quitted my sheltered corner and made my exit by the side-door, which was fortunately near. Thence a narrow passage led into the hall: in crossing it, I perceived my sandal was loose; I stopped to tie it, kneeling down for that purpose on the mat at the foot of the staircase. I heard the dining-room door unclose; a gentleman came out; rising hastily,
> 5 I stood face to face with him: it was Mr Rochester.
> 'How do you do?' he asked.
> 'I am very well, sir.'
> 'Why did you not come and speak to me in the room?'
> I thought I might have retorted the question on him who put it: but I would not take that
> 10 freedom. I answered –
> 'I did not wish to disturb you, as you seemed engaged, sir.'
> 'What have you been doing during my absence?'
> 'Nothing in particular; teaching Adele as usual.'
> 'And getting a great deal paler than you were – as I saw at first sight. What is the matter?'
> 15 'Nothing at all, sir.'
> 'Did you take any cold that night you half drowned me?'
> 'Not the least.'
> 'Return to the drawing-room: you are deserting too early.'
> 'I am tired, sir.'
> 20 He looked at me for a minute.
> 'And a little depressed,' he said. 'What about? Tell me.'
> 'Nothing – nothing. Sir. I am not depressed.'
> 'But I affirm you are: so much depressed that a few more words would bring tears to your eyes – indeed, they are there now, shining and swimming; and a bead has slipped from the
> 25 lash and fallen on the flag. If I had time, and was not in mortal dread of some prating pig of a servant passing, I would know what all this means. Well, tonight I excuse you; but understand that so long as my visitors stay, I expect you to appear in the drawing-room every evening; it is my wish; don't neglect it. Now go, and send Sophie for Adele. Good-night, my – ' He stopped, bit his lip, and abruptly left me.

Starting with this extract, explore about how Brontë writes about Jane's position as a governess and her awareness of social class.

Write about:

- how Brontë writes about Jane's position as a governess in this extract
- how Brontë writes about Jane's position as a governess and her awareness of social class in the novel as a whole.

[30 marks]

5. **Mary Shelley:** *Frankenstein*

Read the following extract from Chapter 4 and then answer the question that follows.

In this extract, Victor Frankenstein describes his work as he begins to create the creature.

> No-one can conceive the variety of feelings which bore me onwards, like a hurricane, in the first enthusiasm of success. Life and death appeared to me ideal bounds, which I should first break through, and pour a torrent of light into our dark world. A new species would bless me as its creator and source; many happy and excellent natures would owe their being
> 5 to me. No father could claim the gratitude of his child so completely as I should deserve theirs. Pursuing these reflections, I thought that if I could bestow animation upon lifeless matter, I might in process of time (although I now found it impossible) renew life where death had apparently devoted the body to corruption.
>
> These thoughts supported my spirits, while I pursued my undertaking with unremitting
> 10 ardour. My cheek had grown pale with study, and my person had become emaciated with confinement. Sometimes, on the very brink of certainty, I failed; yet still I clung to the hope which the next day or the next hour might realize. One secret which I alone possessed was the hope to which I had dedicated myself; and the moon gazed on my midnight labours, while, with unrelaxed and breathless eagerness, I pursued nature to her hiding-places. Who
> 15 shall conceive the horrors of my secret toil as I dabbled among the unhallowed damps of the grave or tortured the living animal to animate the lifeless clay? My limbs now tremble, and my eyes swim with the remembrance; but then a resistless and almost frantic impulse urged me forward; I seemed to have lost all soul or sensation but for this one pursuit. It was indeed but a passing trance, that only made me feel with renewed acuteness so soon as, the unnatural
> 20 stillness ceasing to operate, I had returned to my old habits. I collected bones from charnel-houses and disturbed with profane fingers, the tremendous secrets of the human frame.

Starting with this extract, explore how Shelley writes about Frankenstein's feelings about his work in *Frankenstein*.

Write about:
* how Shelley writes about Frankenstein's feelings about his work in this extract
* how Shelley writes about Frankenstein's feelings about his work in the novel as a whole. **[30 marks]**

6. Jane Austen: *Pride and Prejudice*

Read the following extract from Chapter 29 (vol. 2 Chapter 6) and then answer the question that follows.

In this extract, Mr Collins expresses his delight at receiving an invitation from Lady Catherine de Burgh.

> Mr Collins's triumph in consequence of this invitation was complete. The power of displaying the grandeur of his patroness to his wondering visitors, and of letting them see her civility towards himself and his wife was exactly what he had wished for, and that an opportunity of doing it should be given so soon was an instance of Lady Catherine's
> 5 condescension as he knew not how to admire enough.
>
> 'I confess,' he said, 'that I should not have been at all surprised by her Ladyship's asking us on Sunday to drink tea and spend the evening at Rosings. I rather expected, from my knowledge of her affability, that it would happen. But who could have foreseen such an attention as this? Who could have imagined that we should receive an invitation to dinner
> 10 there (an invitation moreover including the whole party) so immediately after your arrival!'
>
> 'I am the less surprised at what has happened,' replied Sir William, 'from that knowledge of what the manners of the great really are, which my situation in life has allowed me to acquire. About the Court, such instances of elegant breeding are not uncommon.'
>
> Scarcely anything was talked of the whole day or next morning, but their visit to Rosings.
> 15 Mr Collins was carefully instructing them in what they were to expect, that the sight of such rooms, so many servants, and so splendid a dinner might not wholly overpower them.
>
> When the ladies were separating for the toilette, he said to Elizabeth, 'Do not make yourself uneasy, my dear cousin, about your apparel. Lady Catherine is far from requiring that elegance of dress in us, which becomes herself and her daughter. I would advise you merely
> 20 to put on whatever of your clothes is superior to the rest, there is not occasion for anything more. Lady Catherine will not think the worse of you for being simply dressed. She likes to have the distinction of rank preserved.'

Starting with this extract, explore how Austen writes about snobbery in *Pride and Prejudice*.

Write about:
- how Austen writes about snobbery in this extract
- how Austen writes about snobbery in the novel as a whole.   **[30 marks]**

7. **Sir Arthur Conan Doyle: *The Sign of Four***

Read the following extract from Chapter 11 and then answer the question that follows.

In this extract, Watson and Miss Morstan open the box that is supposed to contain the Great Agra Treasure.

'That is all over,' I answered. 'It was nothing. I will tell you no more gloomy details. Let us turn to something brighter. There is the treasure. What could be brighter than that? I got leave to bring it with me, thinking that it would interest you to be the first to see it.'

'It would be of the greatest interest to me,' she said. There was no eagerness in her voice,
5 however. It had struck her, doubtless, that it might seem ungracious upon her part to be indifferent to a prize which had cost so much to win.

'What a pretty box!' she said, stooping over it. 'This is Indian work, I suppose?'

'Yes, it is; Benares metal-work.'

'And so heavy!' she exclaimed, trying to raise it. 'The box alone must be of some value.
10 Where is the key?'

'Small threw it into the Thames,' I answered. 'I must borrow Mrs Forrester's poker.' There was in the front a thick and broad hasp, wrought in the image of a sitting Buddha. Under this I thrust the end of the poker and twisted it outward as a lever. The hasp sprang open with a loud snap. With trembling fingers I flung back the lid. We both stood gazing in astonishment.
15 The box was empty!

No wonder that it was heavy. The iron-work was two thirds of an inch thick all round. It was massive, well made, and solid, like a chest constructed to carry things of great price, but not one shred or crumb of metal or jewellery lay within it. It was absolutely and completely empty.
20 'The treasure is lost,' said Miss Morstan calmly.

As I listened to the words and realized what they meant, a great shadow seemed to pass from my soul. I did not know how this Agra treasure had weighed me down, until now that it was finally removed. It was selfish, no doubt, disloyal, wrong, but I could realize nothing save that the golden barrier was gone from between us.

Starting with this extract, explore how Conan Doyle writes about wealth and its effect on people in *The Sign of Four*.

Write about:
* how Conan Doyle writes about the treasure in this extract
* how Conan Doyle writes about the treasure and wealth in general in the novel as a whole.

[30 marks]

English Literature Paper 2: Modern Prose or Drama

Section A

Answer one question from this section on the text you have studied.

You should spend between 45 and 50 minutes on the question.

N.B. In the exam you will be given a choice of two questions to choose from.

1. **JB Priestley: *An Inspector Calls***

   How does Priestley write about the role and significance of Inspector Goole in *An Inspector Calls?*

   Write about:
   - the role and significance of Inspector Goole
   - how Priestley presents the Inspector.

   [30 marks]
   AO4 [4 marks]

2. **Willy Russell: *Blood Brothers***

   How does Russell write about the character of Linda and her relationship with Mickey and Edward in *Blood Brothers?*

   Write about:
   - the character of Linda and her relationship with Mickey and Edward
   - how Russell presents Linda and her relationship with Mickey and Edward.

   [30 marks]
   AO4 [4 marks]

3. **Alan Bennett: *The History Boys***

   How does Bennett write about friendships between teachers and pupils in *The History Boys?*

   Write about:
   - the friendships between teachers and pupils in the play
   - how Bennett presents these friendships.

   [30 marks]
   AO4 [4 marks]

4. **Dennis Kelly: *DNA***

How does Kelly write about young people's morality (or lack of morality) in *DNA*?

Write about:
- the moral choices made by the young people in *DNA*
- how Kelly presents their moral choices in the play.

[30 marks]
AO4 [4 marks]

5. **Simon Stephens: *The Curious Incident of the Dog in the Night-Time***

How does Stephens write about the ways in which Christopher changes as a result of the death of Wellington in *The Curious Case of the Dog in the Night-Time*?

Write about:
- the ways in which Christopher changes after the death of Wellington
- how Stephens presents these changes.

[30 marks]
AO4 [4 marks]

6. **Shelagh Delaney: *A Taste of Honey***

How docs Delaney write about motherhood in *A Taste of Honey*?

Write about:
- different ideas about motherhood in the play
- how Delaney presents these ideas.

[30 marks]
AO4 [4 marks]

7. **William Golding:** *Lord of the Flies*

How does Golding write about the idea of 'Britishness' in *Lord of the Flies*?

Write about:
- ideas about being British seen in the novel
- how Golding presents these ideas.

[30 marks]
AO4 [4 marks]

8. **AQA Anthology:** *Telling Tales*

How do writers explore how people change in 'The Darkness Out There' and one other story from *Telling Tales*?

Write about:
- how people change in the two stories
- how the writers present these changes.

[30 marks]
AO4 [4 marks]

9. **George Orwell:** *Animal Farm*

How does Orwell write about the pigs becoming more like humans and the reaction of the other animals to this in *Animal Farm*?

Write about:
- how the pigs become more like humans as the novel progresses and the reaction of other animals to this
- how Orwell presents the way the pigs change and the reaction of other animals.

[30 marks]
AO4 [4 marks]

10. **Kazuo Ishiguro: *Never Let Me Go***

How does Ishiguro write about what it means to be human in *Never Let Me Go*?

Write about:
- ideas about what it means to be human put forward in the novel
- how Ishiguro presents these ideas.

[30 marks]
AO4 [4 marks]

11. **Meera Syal: *Anita and Me***

How does Syal write about Meena and her family's feelings about Tollington in *Anita and Me*?

Write about:
- how Meena and her family feel about Tollington
- how Syal presents these feelings.

[30 marks]
AO4 [4 marks]

12. **Stephen Kelman: *Pigeon English***

How does Kelman present female characters in *Pigeon English*?

Write about:
- examples of female characters in *Pigeon English*
- how Kelman presents female characters.

[30 marks]
AO4 [4 marks]

English Literature Paper 2: Poetry and Unseen Poetry

Section B: Poetry

AQA Anthology: *Poems Past and Present*

You should spend between 40 and 45 minutes on this question.

EITHER

1. Compare the way poets use images of nature to convey feelings in 'Winter Swans' and one other poem from 'Love and Relationships'. **[30 marks]**

Winter Swans

The clouds had given their all –
two days of rain and then a break
in which we walked,

the waterlogged earth
gulping for breath at our feet
as we skirted the lake, silent and apart,

until the swans came and stopped us
with a show of tipping in unison.
As if rolling weights down their bodies to their heads

they halved themselves in the dark water
icebergs of white feather, paused before returning again
like boats righting in rough weather.

'They mate for life' you said as they left,
porcelain over the stilling water. I didn't reply
but as we moved on through the afternoon light,

slow-stepping in the lake's shingle and sand,
I noticed our hands, that had, somehow,
swum the distance between us

and folded, one over the other,
like a pair of wings settling after flight.

Owen Sheers

OR

2. Compare the way poets write about how people are changed by experience in 'Remains' and one other poem from 'Power and Conflict'.

[30 marks]

Remains

On another occasion, we got sent out
to tackle looters raiding a bank.
And one of them legs it up the road,
probably armed, possibly not.

Well myself and somebody else and somebody else
are of the same mind,
so all three of us open fire.
Three of a kind all letting fly, and I swear

I see every round as it rips through his life –
I see broad daylight on the other side.
So we've hit this looter a dozen times
and he's there on the ground, sort of inside out,

pain itself, the image of agony.
One of my mates goes by
and tosses his guts back into his body.
Then he's carted off in the back of a lorry.

End of story, except not really.
His blood-shadow stays on the street, and out on patrol
I walk right over it week after week.
Then I'm home on leave. But I blink

and he bursts again through the doors of the bank.
Sleep, and he's probably armed, and possibly not.
Dream, and he's torn apart by a dozen rounds.
And the drink and the drugs won't flush him out-

he's here in my head when I close my eyes,
dug in deep behind the lines,
not left for dead in some distant, sun-stunned, sand-smothered land
or six-feet-under in desert sand,

but near to the knuckle, here and now,
his bloody life in my bloody hands.

Simon Armitage

Section C: Unseen Poetry

Answer both questions in this section.

You should spend a total of between 40 and 50 minutes on both questions.

The Darkling Thrush

I leant upon a coppice gate
    When Frost was spectre-gray,
And Winter's dregs made desolate
    The weakening eye of day.
The tangled bine-stems scored the sky
    Like strings of broken lyres,
And all mankind that haunted nigh
    Had sought their household fires.

The land's sharp features seemed to me
    The Century's corpse outleant,
Its crypt the cloudy canopy,
    The wind its death-lament.
The ancient pulse of germ and birth
    Was shrunken hard and dry,
And every spirit upon earth
    Seemed fervourless as I.

At once a voice arose among
    The bleak twigs overhead
In a full-hearted evensong
    Of joy illimited;
An aged thrush, frail, gaunt and small,
    With blast-beruffled plume,
Had chosen thus to fling his soul
    Upon the growing gloom.

So little cause for carolings
    Of such ecstatic sound
Was written on terrestrial things
    Afar or nigh around,
That I could think there trembled through
    His happy goodnight air
Some blessed Hope, whereof he knew,
    And I was unaware.

Thomas Hardy

1. In 'The Darkling Thrush' how does the poet use natural imagery to present his mood and feelings? **[24 marks]**

> **Spellbound**
>
> The night is darkening round me,
> The wild winds coldly blow;
> But a tyrant spell has bound me
> And I cannot, cannot go.
>
> The giant trees are bending
> Their bare boughs weighed with snow.
> And the storm is fast descending,
> And yet I cannot go.
>
> Clouds beyond clouds above me,
> Wastes beyond wastes below;
> But nothing drear can move me;
> I will not, cannot go.
>
> **Emily Jane Brontë**

2. In both 'The Darkling Thrush' and 'Spellbound' the poets write about nature and their own feelings.

   What are the similarities and/or differences between the ways the poets present nature and their feelings? **[8 marks]**

END OF QUESTIONS

*For answers worth 8 marks or more, detailed mark schemes are given, which include the skills shown in your answer and examples of content you might have included. **They are not full or model answers.** Look at the mark schemes and decide which description is closest to your answer. The number of marks and approximate grade are given.*

English Language Set A

Pages 4–7: Explorations in Creative Reading and Writing

1. **Any four from:** he works in a bar (in the Bowery); he is visiting the doctor/he is not well; he starts work at eight o'clock; he goes for long walks in Central Park (at five in the morning); he is originally from Ireland/ Ireland is his home; he agrees with the doctor that he should visit Ireland. **[1 mark for each up to a maximum of 4]**

2. **[Maximum 8 marks]**

Marks	Skills	Example of Possible Content
7–8 (Grade 7–9)	You have: analysed the use of language; chosen an appropriate range of examples; used a range of subject terminology accurately.	The writer describes Duncannon through the lens of the protagonist's memories. What is described is not what Bryden sees now (he has not yet arrived at Duncannon) but what he 'could see' in his mind's eye. He starts with a topographical explanation of the village's location 'among the rocks of the large headland' before listing its features without the embellishment of adverbs or figurative imagery. He then moves on to a list of the villagers' activities, using a series of present participles and ending with a particular memory, made more vivid by the use of a name and a direct object: 'Michael Malia building a wall'.
5–6 (Grade 5–6)	You have: clearly explained the effect of language choices; chosen relevant examples; used subject terminology accurately.	The writer starts by giving us information, in a very straightforward way, about where the village is and describes the peaceful surroundings of the lake. Then he gives a list of what is in the village. Mentioning the 'Georgian mansion' makes him think of the people who lived there. He makes everyone sound friendly – they were 'boys together' – and hard-working, using verbs like 'mowing, reaping, digging'. He moves from describing a general scene to one person.
3–4 (Grade 3–4)	You have: tried to comment on the effect of language; chosen some relevant examples; used some subject terminology, not always accurately.	He gives a list of what he can see: 'the houses and the streets, and the fields'. He talks about all the jobs that the 'villagers' used to do in the past and it is 'as clear as if it were yesterday' to him.
1–2 (Grade 1–2)	You have: commented in a simple way on language; given simple examples; mentioned subject terminology.	He describes the village using words like 'houses' and 'fields'.

3. [Maximum 8 marks]

Marks	Skills	Example of Possible Content
7–8 (Grade 7–9)	You have: analysed the effects of the choice of structural features; used an appropriate range of quotations; used sophisticated subject terminology appropriately.	In the first paragraph, the reported speech quickly establishes the protagonist's situation, as well as the location in America where the story begins. ('Bowery'…'Central Park'). The following two lines of direct speech and the doctor's suggestion that the (still unnamed) protagonist should go to Ireland, from where he will return a 'new man', lead to the inciting incident: his decision to go 'home'. The sudden change of location, from New York to Ireland, that follows suggests that there will be great change in Bryden. This is underlined by the change of focus to his memories of his earlier life in Ireland, 'as clear as if it were yesterday', seen entirely from his point of view but reported by the omniscient third person narrator. This gives us an insight into his background and conveys a sense of the nostalgia he is feeling. When he leaves the train at Duncannon we get more detail of life in his home village and other characters are introduced. The boy's reported speech gives a sense of the contrast between Duncannon and Bryden's new life in New York. The story of Mike Scully causes Bryden and the reader to question whether he did the right thing in emigrating and starts him thinking about possibly staying in Ireland. The dialogue that ends the extract gives an observer's view of the protagonist, taking us back to the beginning of the story as Mike's judgement that he is 'sallow' reminds us of the visit to the doctor. The extract finishes on a friendly note as Mike wishes him a 'thousand welcome', suggesting that Bryden has indeed come 'home' and is likely to benefit from the experience.
5–6 (Grade 5–6)	You have: clearly explained the effects of structural features; used a range of relevant quotations; used subject terminology appropriately.	The story opens in New York but within a few lines the protagonist is in Ireland. The description of the bar contrasts with later descriptions of the countryside of Ireland and the village of Duncannon. The writer does not tell us much about the man while he is in America, not even his name, just using the third person pronoun 'he'. He reveals something about his feelings through the dialogue with the doctor but it is when he is in Ireland that we start to share his thoughts. We find out about his childhood as well as some details of life in rural Ireland. We also get a sense that he is nostalgic. When he meets Mike Scully the writer shows us how much he has changed as Mike does not know him at first, but the direct speech between them reminds us of the beginning, implying that the doctor was right and that the 'sallow' Bryden might gain physically and psychologically from being welcomed back home.
3–4 (Grade 3–4)	You have: commented on the effect of structure; used some relevant quotations; used some subject terminology, not always appropriately.	The writer starts by describing Bryden in New York. He does not say what is wrong with him but the doctor says 'a sea voyage is what you want' so it does not sound that serious. The focus changes to Ireland and the train journey, where Bryden sees how different life is from New York. It then focuses on the village and Bryden finding out what has happened since he left. This leads to the introduction of a new character, Mike Scully. Mike thinks he is 'a fine man' but 'sallow'. We are left wondering if he will get better in Ireland and maybe even stay there.
1–2 (Grade 1–2)	You have: tried to comment on the effect of structure; referred to the text; mentioned subject terminology.	The character James goes to the doctor's. The doctor tells him go to Ireland and he does. The writer describes what he sees and we know he is the main character. He finds out about changes in the village and meets Mike Scully. We want to find out what happens next.

Answers

4. [Maximum 20 marks]

Marks	Skills	Example of Possible Content
16–20 (Grade 7–9)	You have: critically evaluated the text in a detailed way; used examples from the text to explain your views convincingly; analysed a range of writer's methods; developed a convincing response to the focus of the statement.	The writer tells us very little about Bryden's appearance: when he finally meets Mike Scully we are told through their dialogue of his 'great width of chest' and 'sallow' complexion, giving mixed messages about his health. This relates to earlier in the text where Mike had visited the doctor with an imprecise complaint. That the doctor's advice was to go to Ireland suggests his problems might be psychological as much as physical. However, the reference to his 'sallow complexion' might indicate an illness that is the result of an unhealthy environment in New York. The contrast between how easily he remembers walking from the station to the village and how he now 'does not feel strong enough', vividly reinforces this impression. These problems are likely to inspire sympathy in the reader, while the lack of detail arouses the reader's curiosity. It is a third person narrative but is told mostly from Bryden's point of view. The village and its surroundings are seen through the eyes of a returning emigrant. In some ways, Bryden could be the archetypical Irish emigrant. However, although he is an object of curiosity for the boy, who 'plied him with questions', he answers 'rapidly', suggesting that he is not keen to boast about his experiences – as might be expected from a returning emigrant. The writer does not tell us what his answers are, possibly because the details of his life in America are not relevant to the story or perhaps because he is keeping them back to be revealed later, further intriguing the reader. Bryden is more interested in what has been happening in the village. Although Bryden's memories are rather vague, shown when he has difficulty recalling Mike Scully, news of Mike inspires a 'reverie' (a noun suggesting fantasy, which makes the reader think that he is looking for something unattainable) about what his life might have been had he not emigrated. The general impression is of someone whose experience of emigration has not been positive and whose hopes for the future are rooted not in reality, but in a sentimental idea of what might have been, a character whose situation arouses sympathy and whose uncertain future arouses curiosity.
11–15 (Grade 5–6)	You have: clearly evaluated the text; used examples from the text to explain your views clearly; clearly explained the effect of the writer's methods; made a clear and relevant response to the focus of the statement.	Bryden has come from America because he is ill. He has come to Ireland for a cure but we are not told from what. His attitude to his old home is nostalgic as he thinks about how things were when he left and how they might have changed. The story is told in the third person, making us sympathise with Bryden, but we are not given a lot of detail about his thoughts and feelings. Mike gives us an ambiguous message. He remarks that Bryden is 'a fine man' with a 'great width of chest', so he must be strong, but he also says he is 'sallow in the cheeks' suggesting he is not healthy and reminding us of the visit to the doctor. This gives the impression that New York has not been good for him. His own 'reverie' about a possible life in Ireland and his interest in what has happened to Mike suggest that emigrating has been a disappointment and he is sentimental about life in Ireland. Readers would want to know whether he can achieve his dream of a better life.
6–10 (Grade 3–4)	You have: tried to comment on the text; given an example from the text to explain your views; tried to comment on the writer's methods; made some response to the focus of the statement.	We already know he is now sick. He is very keen to see his home again but he cannot walk from the station, so he must be sick or he is a lot older than when he left. The boy is curious about his life in America but he answers 'rapidly' so he obviously does not want to show off. He seems to be jealous of how Mike Scully's life has worked out. Mike calls him 'a fine man' so he must be strong even though he is 'thin in the cheeks'. The reader feels sorry for him and wants to know what happens next.

Answers

1–5 (Grade 1–2)	You have: made simple comments on the text; given a simple example from the text; mentioned the writer's methods; made a simple response to the focus of the statement.	Mike is sick and lives in the Bowery but he has come back to Ireland. The writer tells us this. He is pleased to be back 'home' and asks all about what has been happening. Then he meets Mike Scully. The reader wants to read on.

5. (a) and **(b)** [Maximum 40 marks]
Content and Organisation [Maximum 24 marks]

22–24 marks (Grade 8–9)	**Content:** You have communicated convincingly and compellingly throughout; your tone, style and register assuredly match purpose, form and audience; you have used an extensive and ambitious vocabulary with sustained crafting of linguistic devices. **Organisation:** Your writing is highly structured and developed, including a range of integrated and complex ideas; your paragraphs are fluently linked with integrated discourse markers; you have used a variety of structural features in an inventive way.
19–21 marks (Grade 7)	**Content:** You have communicated convincingly; your tone, style and register consistently match purpose, form and audience; you have used an extensive vocabulary with evidence of conscious crafting of linguistic devices. **Organisation:** Your writing is structured and developed, including a range of engaging complex ideas; you have used paragraphs consistently with integrated discourse markers; you have used a variety of structural features effectively.
16–18 marks (Grade 6)	**Content:** You have communicated clearly and effectively; your tone, style and register match purpose, form and audience; you have used an increasingly sophisticated vocabulary with a range of appropriate linguistic devices. **Organisation:** Your writing is engaging, including a range of engaging, detailed, connected ideas; you have used paragraphs coherently with integrated discourse markers; you have used structural features effectively.
13–15 marks (Grade 5)	**Content:** You have communicated clearly; your tone, style and register generally match purpose, form and audience; you have used vocabulary for effect with a range of linguistic devices. **Organisation:** Your writing is engaging, including a range of connected ideas; you have usually used paragraphs coherently with a range of discourse markers; you have usually used structural features effectively.
10–12 marks (Grade 4)	**Content:** You have communicated mostly successfully; you have tried to match tone, style and register to purpose, form and audience; you have used vocabulary consciously and used some linguistic devices. **Organisation:** Your writing includes linked and relevant ideas; you have sometimes used paragraphs and discourse markers; you have used some structural features.
7–9 marks (Grade 3)	**Content:** You have communicated with some success; you have tried to match register to purpose, form and audience; you have begun to vary vocabulary and used some linguistic devices. **Organisation:** Your writing includes some linked and relevant ideas; you have tried to write in paragraphs with some discourse markers, not always successfully; you have tried to use structural features.
4–6 marks (Grade 2)	**Content:** You have communicated your ideas; you have shown a simple awareness of purpose, form and audience; you have used a simple vocabulary and simple linguistic devices. **Organisation:** Your writing includes one or two relevant ideas, simply linked; you have tried to write in paragraphs, but the result is random; you have tried to use simple structural features.
1–3 marks (Grade 1)	**Content:** You have communicated some meaning; you have shown an occasional sense of purpose, form and audience; you have used a simple vocabulary. **Organisation:** Your writing includes one or two unlinked ideas; you have not written in paragraphs; you may have tried to use simple structural features.

Technical Accuracy [Maximum 16 marks]

13–16 marks (Grade 7–9)	You have: consistently demarcated sentences accurately; used a wide range of punctuation with a high level of accuracy; used a full range of sentence forms for effect; used Standard English consistently and accurately with secure control of grammatical structures; achieved a high level of accuracy in spelling, including ambitious vocabulary and your use of vocabulary is extensive and sophisticated.

9–12 marks (Grade 5–6)	You have: usually demarcated sentences accurately; used a range of punctuation, usually accurately; used a variety of sentence forms for effect; used Standard English appropriately with control of grammatical structures; spelled most words, including complex and irregular words, correctly and your use of vocabulary is increasingly sophisticated.
5–8 marks (Grade 3–4)	You have: usually demarcated sentences securely; used a range of punctuation, sometimes accurately; tried to use a variety of sentence forms; used some Standard English with some control of agreement; spelled some complex and irregular words correctly; used a varied vocabulary.
1–4 marks (Grade 1–2)	You have: occasionally demarcated sentences; used some punctuation; used a simple range of sentence forms; occasionally used Standard English with limited control of agreement; spelled basic words correctly; used a simple vocabulary.

(a) There are many possible responses. Here is an example of part of a possible answer:

Suddenly a massive edifice of stone appears through the mist. A landscape that seemed deserted as we rowed steadily, carefully, unseeing across the lough – the only sound the regular splish-splash of our innocent oars – is now dominated by this ancient fortress. It is beautiful, but its beauty is cold and forbidding. How long has it stood sentinel over these dark waters? How long has it stood proud among the rolling hills, a symbol of man's power? How long has it stood witness to the ebb and flow of human history?

(b) There are many possible responses. Here is an example of part of a possible answer:

I sat on the park bench and thought about what the doctor had said. Good news. I should have been elated. I could have celebrated: leapt for joy; turned cartwheels; fallen to the ground and sobbed for joy. But I felt nothing. Well, not exactly nothing. I felt (and I don't know how to put this without causing offence) disappointed. I knew this was not how I should be feeling and I resisted it – at first. But it came like a great wave and knocked me off my feet. Then came another wave, a darker, more sinister wave. A new feeling overwhelmed me and I let myself drown in it. It was fear.

Pages 8–12: Writers' Viewpoints and Perspectives

1. A D F G. **[Maximum 4 marks – if more than 4 boxes are shaded 0 marks should be given]**
2. **[Maximum 8 marks]**

Marks	Skills	Example of Possible Content
7–8 (Grade 7–9)	You have: given a perceptive interpretation of both texts; synthesised evidence from the texts; used appropriate quotations from both texts.	Both Lucy's mill and Archie's bakery are praised by the writers but are very different places. Lucy's is highly mechanised and is 'one of the largest' mills in Birmingham, producing ten times the amount of bread that Archie's produces. Archie's 'real bread' methods of doing everything by hand might be a reaction to firms like Lucy's. The bread itself is basically the same, made of 'flour, and water, and yeast, and salt'. However, Archie produces a variety of 'the finest artisan breads' whereas the article about Lucy's does not mention any variety. The only other thing they sell is flour, while Archie's also has cakes and pastries. Lucy's does not sell direct to people but delivers to 'hucksters' shops'. Archie's is a single shop that people come to but they do deliver locally.
5–6 (Grade 5–6)	You have: started to interpret both texts; shown clear connections between texts; used relevant quotations from both texts.	Lucy's is a huge bread mill, 'one of the largest' in Birmingham, making 2000 loaves but Archie's is 'a village bakery' making about 200. He makes his bread 'by hand' but Lucy's uses machines powered by steam. Lucy's sells flour and bread to shops, while Archie sells bread and 'fabulous choux pastry' in his own shop.
3–4 (Grade 3–4)	You have: tried to infer from one/both texts; tried to link evidence between texts; used some quotations from both texts.	Lucy's is one of six 'large bread mills' in Birmingham. Everything is done using 'steam'. Archie does not use machines – 'it's all done by hand'. Lucy's makes a lot more bread than Archie's.
1–2 (Grade 1–2)	You have: paraphrased texts but have not inferred; made simple or no links between texts; referred to one/both texts.	The first one says there is a new mill in Birmingham. The second is about Archie's artisan bread.

3. [Maximum 12 marks]

Marks	Skills	Example of Possible Content
10–12 (Grade 7–9)	You have: analysed the effects of the choice of language; used an appropriate range of quotations; used sophisticated subject terminology appropriately.	The writer tries to engage readers by using informal language ('Hi') and personalising his business, using first and second person pronouns constantly to involve us, as well as repeating his and his wife's names. This could be seen as being friendly (first name terms) but also establishes the couple as a 'brand'. Fabienne's name is shortened to 'Fab', as is the word 'fabulous', contributing to the relentlessly positive (almost boastful) feeling of the piece. Archie's aim is to appear like one of us ('local lad') but also superior because of his experience, training in Paris with 'artisan bakers' and his skills: he is a 'master baker'. This is reinforced by the specialised language he uses: 'fermentation … kneading'. In contrast with his insistence on being 'local' he likes to show off the French connection, using words like 'boulangerie'.
7–9 (Grade 5–6)	You have: clearly explained the effects of the choice of language; used a range of relevant quotations; used subject terminology appropriately.	The tone is quite informal and friendly. The first part is very personal with repetition of the first person pronouns 'I' and 'we' making us think Archie is talking to us personally. Then he explains things in detail and uses technical terms like 'sourdough' to impress us with his expertise. He also uses French words like 'patissiere', maybe because his wife is French but maybe because snobbish people like French things and think they're better. He keeps repeating words like 'local' and 'artisan' to get the message across that he is special.
4–6 (Grade 3–4)	You have: tried to comment on the effect of language; used some relevant quotations; used some subject terminology, not always appropriately.	It is informal and he writes as if he wants to know you, using pronouns 'I' and 'we' and giving a list of what he and his wife have done. He says technical things about the bread, using words like 'starter' and 'sourdough' so you know he's an expert.
1–3 (Grade 1–2)	You have: commented on the effect of language; referred to text; mentioned subject terminology.	The language is friendly. He says 'Hi' and uses words like 'I' and 'we'.

4. [Maximum 16 marks]

Marks	Skills	Example of Possible Content
13–16 (Grade 7–9)	You have: compared ideas and perspectives in a perceptive way; analysed methods used to convey ideas and perspectives; used a range of appropriate quotations.	The two sources have different purposes. Dodd wants his readers to understand how bread is made and how the manufacturers could improve production. His piece is like an academic paper, quoting a French report on the industry and describing processes in London, Paris and Birmingham. Archie also explains bread-making but he wants to drum up business for his own small bakery. He thinks on a much smaller scale. Some of the terminology is similar and both obviously understand the subject. They both use the words 'mix/mixing' and 'knead/kneading' and describe the same basic ingredients. However, they have opposite points of view on mechanising the bread-making process. To Dodd, the traditional way of bread-making he has observed is 'rude and primitive', making the 'uncouthness' of the bakers seem revolting and unhygienic. To him, steam mills and other machines can only be an improvement. Archie, writing over 150 years later, says he 'bakes… with the heart' and, by using terms like 'real bread', implies that there is something false and unhealthy about bread produced in factories.

Marks	Skills	Example of Possible Content
9–12 (Grade 5–6)	You have: compared ideas and perspectives in a clear and relevant way; explained clearly methods used to convey ideas and perspectives; used relevant quotations from both texts.	Source A is about the way bread is made in the 1850s and looks at how it can be improved. The writer thinks making bread by hand is inefficient. He uses words like 'clumsily', 'straddling and wriggling' and 'uncouthness', which all make it seem unpleasant. In contrast, the big steam mills in Birmingham seem much better. Source B, however, rejects 'white sliced pre-packaged bread' and wants to go back to doing everything by hand. He paints a picture of everything being done properly in a nice family environment. He is not interested in producing huge amounts of bread.
5–8 (Grade 3–4)	You have: identified some differences between ideas and perspectives; commented on methods used to convey ideas and perspectives; used some quotations from one or both texts.	Dodd explains in detail how bread is made in Paris. He does not think it should be done like this but would like them to use machines. This is 'progress' and he gives examples of big mills in Birmingham where they use machines and make 2000 loaves a day. Archie is the opposite. He is proud of making a small amount of bread 'by hand'. He calls it 'real bread' and explains what goes into it and who makes it.
1–4 (Grade 1–2)	You have: referred to different ideas and perspectives; identified how differences are conveyed; made simple references to one or both texts.	The first writer says bread-making is very hard work but he thinks it could be easier with machines. Archie does not like machines – 'it's all done by hand'.

5. Look at the mark scheme for question 5 on pages 69–70. This task is marked for content and organisation, and for technical accuracy. **[Maximum 40 marks]**
There are many possible responses. Here is an example of part of a possible answer:
Recently, I watched a programme on television about British families' eating habits. It was primarily concerned with budgeting but also looked at nutrition and healthy eating. On it a young woman, the mother of the family, declared (in all seriousness) that she bought expensive, processed cheese slices because it takes so long to slice cheese! I accept that she led a busy life, with a full-time job, two children and a house to look after, but surely nobody is too busy to slice cheese.

This was just one of many examples of people wasting money on often unhealthy processed foods when fresh produce, bought more cheaply and prepared at home – as the woman in question discovered – is not only better for us physically but can also help to give us a better quality of family life. How? Far from being a waste of time, cooking can be relaxing and enjoyable. It is also something families can do together, bringing them closer as they work towards a shared goal.

English Language Set B

Pages 14–18: Explorations in Creative Reading and Writing

1. **Any four from:** the open square; the tops of the trees; a peddler; someone singing; sparrows; patches of blue sky
[1 mark for each up to a maximum of 4]
2. **[Maximum 8 marks]**

Marks	Skills	Example of Possible Content
7–8 (Grade 7–9)	You have: analysed the effects of the choice of language; used an appropriate range of quotations; used sophisticated subject terminology appropriately.	The omniscient narrator, describing Louise's appearance and her personality, uses language that suggests a lack of passion. She is 'calm' and has a 'dull stare' with her look indicating 'a suspension of intelligent thought'. From this, the reader might think she was stunned by her news or just unfeeling but the references to 'repression' and 'a certain strength' alert us to something going on under the surface. Chopin uses an extended metaphor to convey how she discovers her true feelings. They could be a monster 'creeping … reaching', the present participles here giving a sense of movement and danger. Her reaction is expressed using the kind of violent vocabulary one might expect in a horror story. 'Her bosom rose and fell tumultuously' suggests she is being physically attacked and the use of the verb 'to possess' could suggest rape, as does the feminine powerlessness of her 'white slender hands', which provide a simile for her weak 'will'.

5–6 (Grade 5–6)	You have: clearly explained the effects of language; used a range of relevant quotations; used subject terminology appropriately.	At first words like 'calm', 'dull' and 'gaze' suggest that she is not really upset about her husband's death and is perhaps a bit stupid. But then her feelings change and there are a lot of violent words like the adverb 'tumultuously' and the phrase 'beat it back'. We do not know what she is fighting but by using the imagery of something attacking Louise, Chopin conveys how frightened she is and how much this 'creeping' feeling could affect her.
3–4 (Grade 3–4)	You have: commented on the effect of language; used some relevant quotations; used some subject terminology, not always appropriately.	She seems not to be feeling much because she has a 'dull stare'. She thinks something frightening is going to happen, using metaphors as if it is an animal 'creeping'.
1–2 (Grade 1–2)	You have: tried to comment on the effect of language; referred to the text; mentioned subject terminology.	She was young and she was afraid. The writer uses the word 'fearfully' to describe her.

3. **[Maximum 8 marks]**

Marks	Skills	Example of Possible Content
7–8 (Grade 7–9)	You have: analysed the use of structural features; chosen an appropriate range of examples; used a range of subject terminology accurately.	The writer quickly introduces the situation and characters, briefly alluding to Louise's health. Brently's death is a shocking event. The reader would expect the story to focus on Louise's reaction and how she might cope. As the focus shifts to Louise, alone in her room, the writer explores her feelings and there is a turning point when she and the reader realise that her life will change but not in the way they might have expected. The mood changes with the protagonist's mood to one of hope and expectation. The next turning point, the unexpected entrance of Louise's husband, is shocking and dashes all her hopes. It seems like the end but Chopin plays a trick on the reader. The story is not really over. The reader might have forgotten the opening sentence about Louise's 'heart trouble' but now it creates the 'sting in the tail' with the short penultimate sentence – 'But Richards was too late' – stunning the reader before the final sentence economically explains what has happened and leaves us with an ambiguous and ironic sentiment.
5–6 (Grade 5–6)	You have: clearly explained the effect of structural features; chosen relevant examples; used subject terminology accurately.	The story starts with Louise hearing the news of her husband's death. The focus is on how people break the news to her and how it has happened before switching to Louise's reaction, which is not 'as many women' would have reacted but still quite normal. Then the writer describes Louise alone in her room and how her reaction changes from being stunned to a violent one of being glad she is 'free'. This is a turning point and the writer tells us how her life might be and seems to be a happy ending for her but then there is a shocking twist when her husband walks in. Ironically, it is Louise who ends up dead.
3–4 (Grade 3–4)	You have: tried to comment on structure; chosen some relevant examples; used some subject terminology, not always accurately.	At the beginning, Louise hears about her husband's death. The first surprise is that she 'did not hear the story as many women have'. We wonder what her reaction will be. At first she is 'dull' but then she is glad: 'Free, free, free!' But this is not the last surprise. The twist at the end is that he is not dead and she dies when she hears the news.
1–2 (Grade 1–2)	You have: commented in a simple way on structure; given simple examples; mentioned subject terminology.	At the start, she thinks he is dead. At the end, she finds out he isn't and she dies.

Answers

4. [Maximum 20 marks]

Marks	Skills	Example of Possible Content
16–20 (Grade 7–9)	You have: critically evaluated the text in a detailed way; used examples from the text to explain your views convincingly; analysed a range of writer's methods; developed a convincing and critical response to the focus of the statement.	Louise has been introduced to the reader as someone who is emotionally and physically fragile, suggesting that she needs to be taken care of. This makes what happens in the latter part of the story all the more surprising. Chopin describes her physically, the 'calm' of her face reflecting her mood. We also learn about her 'strength' and the word 'repression' is used, suggesting this is not the woman we thought she was. Her excitement and fear about the 'something coming to her' indicate a massive shift in her life, which could be good or bad, but when she cries 'Free, free, free!' we know that she must see marriage as a prison from which she is about to be liberated. The use of repetition in this exclamation emphasises not only the strength of her emotion but the importance of the adjective 'free' and the concept of liberty. Her later exclamation of 'Free! Body and soul free!' reinforces the centrality of this idea and suggests that marriage is doubly oppressive: physically and spiritually. Louise is clearly dependent on her husband and limited in her choices as a wife. However, Chopin speaks of 'men and women' imposing their 'will upon a fellow-creature', suggesting she sees marriage as prison for both sexes.
11–15 (Grade 5–6)	You have: clearly evaluated the text; used examples from the text to explain your views clearly; clearly explained the effect of the writer's methods; made a clear and relevant response to the focus of the statement.	Louise is described as having 'a certain strength' in contrast to the beginning of the story where her family and friends are shown to be protective of her. It becomes clear that she is not really a weak character. The writer also mentions 'repression' so we feel she does not usually let out her feelings. These feelings change. The description of her 'calm', following her earlier 'wild abandonment', could be seen as a normal stage in the grieving process, although for her it comes very quickly. She must see marriage as a prison as she shouts 'Free, free, free!' – the repetition showing how important the idea of freedom is. Through her the writer explores ideas about women and marriage. She does not look forward to life alone because her marriage is bad – she had loved him – but 'self-assertion' is more important.
6–10 (Grade 3–4)	You have: tried to comment on the text; given an example from the text to explain your views; tried to comment on the writer's methods; made some response to the focus of the statement.	The writer has introduced the character as having heart trouble and the reader will think she is quite weak and delicate. You would think she depended on her husband but the second part of the text gives a different impression. The writer tells us what she is feeling and that she is frightened of something 'creeping out of the sky' so it is strange that she turns out to be happy about his death. She must think of marriage as a bad thing for women. She wants to 'live for herself'.
1–5 (Grade 1-2)	You have: made simple comments on the text; given a simple example from the text; mentioned the writer's methods; made a simple response to the focus of the statement.	She was 'young with a fair calm face'. She is shocked at first but then she shouts out that she is 'free'. She is glad he is dead so she does not like marriage.

5. Look at the mark scheme for question 5 on pages 69–70. This task is marked for content and organisation, and for technical accuracy. **[Maximum 40 marks]**

(a) There are many possible responses. Here is an example of part of a possible answer:

Somewhere, underneath the chaos, lay a beautiful sandy beach surrounded by gentle inclines, embracing clear blue sea. That was what I had been looking forward to that summer's day: peace, tranquillity, relaxation. Unfortunately for me, a thousand others had had the same idea – and here they were. As far as I could see, the beach was covered in striped windbreakers, garish little tents, sun beds and blankets, even a rather forlorn looking ice-cream van – it was surrounded by holidaymakers yet they all but ignored it. Hardly surprising. Summer it might have been but nobody had told the weather. No suncream or bikinis for these would-be sun worshippers. It was a day for cardigans and thermos flasks and making the most of it.

Answers

(b) There are many possible responses. Here is an example of part of a possible answer:

'I think you'd better sit down,' she said. 'I've got some bad news.'

The laughter stopped immediately. We all looked at her. Amy's face betrayed no emotion. Not a flicker of the eyelids. Not a quiver of the lip. She stood, straight-backed and steady, her face immobile as if carved in stone. Sphinx-like. I remembered something Gran had once said about still waters running deep. It made me impatient with Amy and her unnatural calmness.

'Okay, Amy. You've got our attention. Just say what you've got to say and go.'

Pages 19–22: Writers' Viewpoints and Perspectives

1. B C F G. [Maximum 4 – if more than 4 boxes are shaded 0 marks should be given]

2. [Maximum 8 marks]

Marks	Skills	Example of Possible Content
7–8 (Grade 7–9)	You have: given a perceptive interpretation of both texts; synthesised evidence from the texts; used appropriate quotations from both texts.	Both writers describe behaviour they consider to be 'familiarity' (Trollope) or 'over-familiarity' (Boyle). The former criticises the behaviour of a particular neighbour before talking about Americans in general, while the latter mentions waiters, TV presenters and teachers. Trollope acknowledges the woman is helpful and intends to be friendly, and concludes her 'violent intimacy' is the norm in the USA. Boyle does not think the behaviour he describes is genuine and thinks it is copied from an idea of American friendliness. Both are concerned with forms of address. Trollope says that she and her husband are called 'the old man' and 'the English old woman' while ordinary working people such as 'draymen, butchers' boys and labourers' are referred to as ladies and gentlemen. Boyle is concerned with service rather than class and says people in 'service industries' in France and Italy behave properly in contrast with those serving in Britain.
5–6 (Grade 5–6)	You have: started to interpret both texts; shown clear connections between texts; used relevant quotations from both texts.	Trollope writes about the manners of Americans, Boyle about British people who imitate American manners. The behaviour Trollope describes is mostly from a woman who is over friendly, using first names and calling the children 'honey'. Boyle writes mostly about waiters. He says they now say 'You guys' instead of 'Sir/Madam'. He says others, like teachers, do the same thing.
3–4 (Grade 3–4)	You have: tried to infer from one/both texts; tried to link evidence between texts; used some quotations from both texts.	The first is about a neighbour in America who is trying to be friendly. She is 'jovial' and tries to help. The waiters Boyle writes about are also meant to help but they are paid for it and might not really be friendly. They both lack respect.
1–2 (Grade 1–2)	You have: paraphrased texts but have not inferred; made simple or no links between texts; referred to one/both texts.	They both talk about Americans. In the first one she meets a neighbour she does not like. The second is about waiters being rude.

3. [Maximum 12 marks]

Marks	Skills	Example of Possible Content
10–12 (Grade 7–9)	You have: analysed the effects of the choice of language; used an appropriate range of quotations; used sophisticated subject terminology appropriately.	Trollope starts with an anecdote to illustrate her point. She describes the situation in an understated, undramatic way ('absent rather longer than we expected') so it is clear that the search is not in itself the point of the story. Her later use of hyperbole, for example 'exceedingly coarse and vehement' and 'violent intimacy', and the idea that the woman 'almost frightened' her (when you might think she'd be more frightened about her children being missing) suggests she wants to both shock and amuse, as does her reference to the 'amusement' of her children. In the second paragraph she uses a lot of direct speech to give the reader a flavour of American manners. She quotes the dialect of the Americans: 'That there lady… what is making dip-candles'. Here both the juxtaposition of the term 'lady' (in England usually someone who did not work) and 'making dip-candles' and the use of the non-standard 'that there' and 'what is' add both to the vividness of the picture and its humorous tone. Yet the tone seems affectionate, with a hint of self-deprecation, so you do not feel that she is 'making fun' of her neighbours.

Answers

Marks	Skills	Example of Possible Content
7–9 (Grade 5–6)	You have: clearly explained the effects of the choice of language; used a range of relevant quotations; used subject terminology appropriately.	The narrative is formal, with long sentences and formal, old-fashioned standard English: 'our party determined' and 'such a pair had been seen to pass'. When she meets the woman whom she compares to a market woman to give readers an idea of her appearance, her language becomes more dramatic. The woman is 'coarse and vehement' and Trollope does not like her 'violent intimacy'. She wants to put across how Americans speak so she uses a lot of quotations in the second half. Phrases like 'them gentlemen' and 'that there lady' convey both their dialect and their attitude.
4–6 (Grade 3–4)	You have: tried to comment on the effect of language; used some relevant quotations; used some subject terminology, not always appropriately.	She tells the story of looking for her children in long sentences but without much description. The tone is calm so she cannot be panicking: 'They were absent rather longer than we expected'. She quotes a lot of speech from Americans and writes it in a sort of dialect to make it amusing to readers: 'That there lady.'
1–3 (Grade 1–2)	You have: commented on the effect of language; referred to the text; mentioned subject terminology.	She describes people and gives examples of their speech. They speak in an American way.

4. [Maximum 16 marks]

Marks	Skills	Example of Possible Content
13–16 (Grade 7–9)	You have: compared ideas and perspectives in a perceptive way; analysed methods used to convey ideas and perspectives; used a range of appropriate quotations.	The two writers have broadly similar attitudes to manners. They both prefer a degree of formality. Trollope uses the word 'familiarity' and Boyle 'over–familiarity' in the same pejorative way. Trollope is shocked ('almost frightened') by some of the ways of Americans while Boyle is 'outraged' by being addressed in a familiar, American-style way by a waiter. However, Trollope's purpose in writing is to inform her audience of the ways of Americans, remarking that such manners are 'universal' in the USA, while Boyle assumes his audience is familiar with the behaviour he is complaining about. He is putting forward an argument about the Americanisation of manners in Britain and expressing his distaste. Consequently, his tone is one of comic exaggerated outrage ('I would never leave the house'; 'never, ever') mixed with a serious attempt to analyse what he sees. Trollope too uses comedy but she is concerned more with reporting what she sees than analysis.
9–12 (Grade 5–6)	You have: compared ideas and perspectives in a clear and relevant way; explained clearly methods used to convey ideas and perspectives; used relevant quotations from both texts.	The two writers both dislike 'familiarity' and get upset by people being too informal with them. However, in Boyle's case he is only talking about people in 'service industries', while Trollope is talking about Americans in general. Trollope is writing a book about the 'manners' of Americans so we can infer that at that time people in England behaved in a very different way. Boyle's main complaint is that phrases like 'you guys' have been 'imported from America'. He wants us to be different from them. They both use quotations in order to criticise them, and amuse the reader: 'them gentlemen' and 'Listen up, guys'. Boyle is angrier than Trollope, who is just surprised by what she hears.
5–8 (Grade 3–4)	You have: identified some differences between ideas and perspectives; commented on methods used to convey ideas and perspectives; used some quotations from one or both texts.	They do not like 'over–familiarity' and are both bothered about how people talk to them. However, Trollope is talking about the difference between the English and Americans, while Boyle is angry about English people imitating Americans. They both try to use humour, Trollope by using language like 'violent intimacy' and describing her 'dread' of meeting the woman and Boyle by using words like 'touch their forelocks'. Both are a bit snobbish.

1–4 (Grade 1–2)	You have: referred to different ideas and perspectives; identified how differences are conveyed; made simple references to one or both texts.	They both want people to be more polite and they don't like them being friendly. Trollope doesn't like Americans and Boyle doesn't like waiters.

5. Look at the mark scheme for question 5 on pages 68–69. This task is marked for content and organisation, and for technical accuracy. **[Maximum 40 marks]**

There are many possible responses. Here is an example of part of a possible answer:

While it is obvious that no-one can share the same degree of intimacy with all their five hundred Facebook friends, neither can we be equally close to everyone that we know in the 'real' world. The difference surely is in the terminology, not the fact. People we refer to as 'friends' online are not friends in the traditional sense. We call them that because that is what the company that provides our means of communication calls them. They call them that because it sounds warm, positive and, well, friendly. Many of these people are really just acquaintances or contacts. They are the internet equivalent of the neighbour we nod to in the street or the girl we occasionally sit next to in French. However, that does not stop some of them becoming as close as the friends we have grown up with: sharing experiences and secrets; arguing and making up; laughing and crying together.

English Literature Set A

For all Shakespeare, the 19ᵗʰ Century Novel, and Modern Prose or Drama questions, look at the mark scheme below.
[Maximum 30 marks]

Marks	Skills
26–30 (Grade 8–9)	You have: responded to the task in an exploratory and critical way; used precise, appropriate references to support your interpretation; analysed the writer's methods using subject terminology appropriately; explored the effects of the writer's methods; explored links between text and ideas/context.
21–25 (Grade 7)	You have: responded to the task in a thoughtful, developed way; used appropriate references to support your interpretation; examined the writer's methods using subject terminology effectively; examined the effects of the writer's methods; thoughtfully considered links between text and ideas/context.
16–20 (Grade 5–6)	You have: responded to the task in a clear way; used references effectively to support your explanation; clearly explained the writer's methods using relevant subject terminology; understood the effects of the writer's methods; clearly understood links between text and ideas/context.
11–15 (Grade 3–4)	You have: given some explanation of the task; used references to support some comments; explained the writer's methods, sometimes using subject terminology; identified the effects of the writer's methods; understood some links between text and ideas/context.
6–10 (Grade 2)	You have: responded to the task and supported your response; commented on some references; identified the writer's methods; referred to subject terminology; shown awareness of some links between text and ideas/context.
1–5 (Grade 1)	You have: responded to the task with simple comments; referred to some details; shown awareness that the writer has made choices; referred to subject terminology; made a simple comment on ideas/context.

AO4 will be assessed for Section A of Paper 1 (Shakespeare) and Section A of Paper 2 (Modern Prose or Drama)

Marks	Skills
4	You have spelled and punctuated with consistent accuracy, and consistently used vocabulary and sentence structure to achieve control of meaning.
2–3	You have spelled and punctuated with considerable accuracy, and used a considerable range of vocabulary and sentence structures to achieve general control of meaning.
1	You have spelled and punctuated with reasonable accuracy, and used a reasonable range of vocabulary and sentence structures; errors do not hinder meaning.

Answers

Pages 25–30: Shakespeare

Look at the mark scheme on page 77.
[Maximum 30 marks plus 4 marks for AO4]
Your answers could include some of the following points.

1. *Macbeth*
   As he reacts, his speech is broken up by caesuras; he asks a series of short questions, seeming not to believe the news; he accepts Malcolm's advice but asserts he must 'feel it like a man'; the scene gives Macduff the personal motivation to seek revenge; he gains sympathy as a family man and for showing his feelings; earlier he has passed Malcolm's 'test' by showing his own integrity; he is seen as loyal and brave, as Macbeth was at the start of the play; he fights bravely and fiercely and is patriotic and loyal to Malcolm; unlike Macbeth, he is honest and neither cruel nor ambitious; when he kills Macbeth we learn he was 'from his mother's womb/Untimely ripped', so the witches' prophecy can be true.

2. *Romeo and Juliet*
   Friar Laurence is surprised and shocked by Romeo saying he loves Juliet; he sees Romeo (and all young men) as fickle, their love 'not truly in their hearts, but in their eyes'; he recalls how love for Rosaline made Romeo miserable; his old love was read by 'rote', implying it was not real but like something from a story; he distinguishes between 'doting' and 'loving', not believing Romeo truly loved Rosaline; Juliet returns Romeo's love – 'Doth grace for grace and love for love allow'; Friar Laurence might not be convinced but sees an opportunity for reconciling the Capulets and Montagues; Romeo and Juliet's love is seen as strong and mutual when they meet; love is also complete when they marry, giving spiritual and sexual fulfilment; however, it puts them in opposition to their families, leading to their deaths.

3. *The Tempest*
   Caliban does not seem to want freedom, just a different master; he is servile, not defiant as he was before; all the characters are drunk and the scene is broadly comic; however, Caliban unexpectedly speaks in verse and describes the island poetically; perhaps this shows what he could have been if Prospero had not enslaved him – or perhaps his eloquence is the result of the education Prospero gave him; Caliban sings about his freedom. His joy might be genuine but he is not actually free; the play is influenced by the colonisation of places like America going on at the time, with settlers enslaving indigenous peoples; Caliban and Ariel are sometimes seen as two different kinds of slave; Prospero also enslaves Ferdinand to test his love; in a sense, all the characters are imprisoned on the island and most are freed at the end.

4. *Much Ado About Nothing*
   He is Don Pedro's brother but, as a bastard, is an outsider with no power; he claims that he is honest and will not pretend to gain favour; this is the first time we see him – he is talking to his confidant, Conrad, so we can take what he says as the truth; Conrad urges him to co-operate now he has been defeated by Don Pedro; they both use natural imagery – Conrad talks about a 'harvest' but Don John of being 'a canker in a hedge'; we will see later the use he makes of his discontent as he plots against Claudio and Hero; his actions provide the plot of the play, both by causing Claudio to reject Hero and, indirectly, bringing Beatrice and Benedick together; his presence casts a shadow over the play. He stands apart from the happiness of the others at the end; he can be seen as a 'malcontent', an unhappy character at odds with the world, common in plays of the time.

5. *The Merchant of Venice*
   Portia is in control here, telling Bassanio what she wants; however, she is controlled by the will of her dead father; she is obedient to her father's wishes, not wanting to be 'forsworn'; making a good marriage is important to her as well as to her father, but she wants to marry the man she loves; she speaks openly of her love for Bassanio while stating that 'a maiden hath no tongue but thought', meaning she has no real power; Jessica, like Portia, is controlled by her father but she asserts her independence by eloping; Portia and Nerissa disguise themselves as men. This is necessary if Portia is to be taken seriously; all three women express themselves openly and behave independently, following their hearts.

6. *Julius Caesar*
   Brutus's suicide would be seen as honourable by Romans; Antony makes a distinction between Brutus and the others – 'only he' had 'honest' motives; he is seen as a good politician, interested in 'common good to all'; he is also praised as a man – he was 'gentle' and he lacked the vice of envy; Antony uses rhetoric to proclaim Brutus's worth, imagining nature itself praising him; Octavius echoes Antony's sentiments, wanting him treated 'according to his virtue'. Their sentiments are especially important because they were his enemies; in his conversations with Cassius, Brutus is shown as the idealist, an honourable man; he is important to the conspiracy because of his reputation; he is a brave soldier and leader who inspires love and loyalty.

Pages 31–37: The 19th Century Novel

Look at the mark scheme on page 77.
[Maximum 30 marks]
Your answers could include some of the following points.

1. *The Strange Case of Dr Jekyll and Mr Hyde*
   In this chapter Jekyll is the narrator so we see the story from his point of view; he emphasises the potential dangers of the experiment; given the risks and the fact that he is experimenting on himself, the reader might admire Jekyll's actions; the description of the

experiment is cool and factual but not detailed –
no ingredients are named; the second paragraph
focuses on Jekyll's reactions, carefully recorded but
dramatic and disturbing; he brings together the worlds
of science and morality, trying to separate good and
evil; the experiment quickly becomes out of control as
Hyde takes over; although Jekyll is using chemicals
and transforming physically, the novel is more about
psychology; Jekyll could be seen as 'playing God',
interfering with nature in an unacceptable way, which
is bound to end in tragedy.

2. *A Christmas Carol*
Scrooge is reluctant to go with the spirit but is less
aggressive and uncooperative than before; the
ghost is gentle but firm in making Scrooge go with
him; Scrooge wants the ghost to put on his cap not
knowing why – perhaps he is resisting the light of
knowledge; the ghost reassures him that he has come
to help him but Scrooge is nervous. Dickens uses
these scenes to show how experience has changed
Scrooge psychologically – his character the result
of nurture, not nature; his lack of love as a child and
the death of Fan explain his lack of feeling and his
attitude to his nephew; he also made bad choices. He
could have been like Mr Fezziwig as a boss and he
could have married if he had not worshipped money;
other characters, like the Cratchits, are shown not to
be embittered by bad experiences; the ghosts show
Scrooge that he can make choices and change for the
better.

3. *Great Expectations*
The adult Pip is critical of his old ideas: 'I am
afraid…'; he makes his younger self seem ridiculous
for feeling even the stars were 'poor and humble';
Pip is aware of the difference the new clothes might
make to how people look at him; Joe and Biddy have
a different view, wanting to impress people with the
new 'gen-teel' Pip; he dismisses the people of his
own class as 'coarse and common', showing that he
is becoming snobbish; Biddy shows awareness of
his attitudes, almost tricking him into doing the right
thing; his attitude confuses him but he is drawn to
what he sees as a 'better' life; throughout the novel
Pip gets into trouble because of his naïve belief in the
superiority of people from higher social classes; the
reader can see the worth of characters like Joe and
Biddy – representatives of the working class; Dickens
exposes good and bad in all classes as Pip learns
what is really of value in life.

4. *Jane Eyre*
The description of the church gives a sense of
its importance and permanence, the building
representing the idea of religion; Jane is aware of the
significance of everything in the 'quiet and humble
temple', this description reflecting her own nature; the
words of the service about 'impediment' are given
in full; the interruption is shocking and dramatic,
breaking the atmosphere; Rochester is happy to go
ahead in the knowledge that he is deceiving Jane and

their marriage would not be 'lawful'; the fact that this
happens in the church shows the extent of Rochester's
deceit and the chasm between his and Jane's
beliefs; Jane uses the language of religion throughout
the novel and has a strong faith; although she is
independently minded, her behaviour is always guided
by her beliefs; she cannot agree to be Rochester's
mistress because of her moral attitude; she can be
critical of others who profess religious belief, however,
especially if they are hypocrites; the religious fervour
and goodness of St John Rivers are attractive to her
but she realises that she cannot love him or dedicate
herself to missionary work.

5. *Frankenstein*
Frankenstein consciously seeks spiritual comfort or
inspiration in the mountains; the detailed description of
his climb is in the present tense and reads almost like
a travel guide; the place and the weather reflect his
mood – pathetic fallacy – and he is aware of this; there
is a sense of danger in the steep climb, increased by
the bad weather, giving the reader a sense of there
being something dramatic to come; the scene causes
him to reflect on the nature of man; here and elsewhere
the attitude to nature is in the Romantic tradition;
descriptions of the vastness and magnificence of
natural scenes give a sense of there being a power
greater than man, whether God or nature itself;
Frankenstein's experiment can be seen as interfering
with nature in a way that must end in tragedy; the
experiences of the creature focus on nature in a
different sense – the nature vs nurture debate.

6. *Pride and Prejudice*
There is an extreme contrast in the reactions of Mr and
Mrs Bennet; Mrs Bennet saw Mr Collins as a good
match for Elizabeth so she is disappointed; although
expressed in a comic way, getting her daughters
married is a serious issue; Mr Bennet's 'tranquil'
response is more reasonable but reflects his refusal
to take his wife's concerns seriously; seeing Charlotte
as more foolish than his daughter is ironic as, in fact,
Charlotte's decision is sensible and practical; both
parents have favourites – Mr Bennet prefers Elizabeth
to the others; as a father he is loving (at least to
Elizabeth) but rather distant and selfish; Mrs Bennet
is overbearing and embarrassing but sees herself
as working for her daughters' happiness; parent/
child relationships must be seen in the context of the
social and economic position of the girls and their
dependence on their father and their future husbands.

7. *The Sign of Four*
The first person narrative gives immediacy and the
readers see only what Watson sees; the relationship
between the two men provides a light-hearted contrast
to the mystery; Watson reports Holmes's speech,
showing his brilliance and his arrogance; 'A Study in
Scarlet' was Conan Doyle's last novel and Holmes's
reaction to it would amuse readers; Watson shares
his hurt and annoyance with the reader; Watson is
anxious to be valued but Holmes seems unable to

Answers

compliment or flatter him; Holmes's analysis of the small brochure is harsh but honest, contrasting with Watson's false modesty; Watson mentions his wound – his military and medical experience give him credibility as an observer; elsewhere Watson incorporates other characters' narratives; Watson can be seen as representing the average intelligent reader.

Pages 38–39: Modern Prose or Drama

Look at the mark scheme on page 77.
[Maximum 30 marks plus 4 marks for AO4]
Your answers could include some of the following points.

1. *An Inspector Calls*
   Priestley presents a very unequal society – we see the rich middle-class Birlings and hear about Eva Smith; Eva experiences many problems, such as losing her job and getting pregnant; at the time the play is set there is little help for her; Priestley wrote the play in the 1940s when there was a lot of discussion about the welfare state; Eva could be several different girls with different problems; she is a device for bringing them to our attention; her problems can be seen in terms of socialism and/or feminism. Are they the result of her class or her gender?; the central message is about taking responsibility for each other.

2. *Blood Brothers*
   Mrs Johnstone makes a choice to give away (or sell) her child; her choice may be justified by her economic circumstances; there is a sense that tragedy is inevitable, expressed by the narrator; is this because of what she has done or because of class and poverty?; Mickey is seen as the victim of social inequality; however, he makes bad choices throughout the play; the writer's (and audience's) sympathies seem to be entirely with Mrs Johnstone and Mickey; the two boys are not different in nature – their differences are the result of upbringing.

3. *The History Boys*
   The Headmaster sees education as a competition – the boys' success reflects on the school; he is not an academic high-flyer and is in awe of Oxford and Cambridge; he does not give away what he really thinks about issues such as Hector's 'fiddling'; he has a distant relationship with the teachers and pupils. Teachers call him 'Headmaster'; he uses the teachers and manipulates them, especially Irwin against Hector; in turn he is manipulated and controlled by Dakin; his public language is formal and authoritative (as in his last speech) while in private it is coarse; he could be seen as being interested in self-preservation and taking credit for others' efforts.

4. *DNA*
   All the characters are teenagers. We are in their world; the 'killing' of Adam is shocking and shows what they are capable of; their reaction, blaming the postman, might be more shocking; they are part of a gang/friendship group but also belong to smaller groups; the interaction between them and the way

they talk is typically 'teenage' – normal in spite of the abnormality of their actions; their relations with adults are not shown, only reported by them, but seem distant; they are distinct characters with different reactions, so not just stereotypical teenagers; they are dominated by strong characters and the demands of the group.

5. *The Curious Incident of the Dog in the Night-Time*
   'I find people confusing': Christopher articulates his perspective on the world; he speaks differently from other characters, saying what he thinks without embellishment; other characters are conscious of treating him differently, e.g. not touching him; his relationship with Siobhan marks him out as 'officially' different as in having special needs; his parents demonstrate how his 'difference' affects those close to him; his thoughts are presented through Siobhan reading his notes; the way he experiences life is presented theatrically, e.g. by the voices when he arrives at the station.

6. *A Taste of Honey*
   The play is centred on Jo and Helen, the men being incidental characters; Jo's relationships with men may be a reaction to her mother's attitudes; Helen uses men for money and sex. She depends on them but does not respect them; Jo's relationship with the boy is romantic but brief; he lets her down, shattering her dreams; the boy and Geof are outsiders (like Jo), one because of race and the other because of sexuality; Peter, the one man who is not an outsider, is unpleasant and overbearing; all the men leave Jo in the end, leaving her with Helen and facing an independent but uncertain future.

7. *Lord of the Flies*
   Simon is the opposite of Jack. He is inherently good; He is gentle, and kind to the little 'uns; he has the same sort of background as the other boys but for him ideas about morality and civilisation are not superficial; he understands what the 'beast' means; his hallucinations are almost mystical and holy; His murder represents the ultimate triumph of evil and savagery; he can be seen as a sacrificial victim, perhaps like Jesus.

8. *Telling Tales*
   At first the narrator seems to have a good relationship with his father as they go fishing together; they co-operate and work well together; fishing is part of a disappearing way of life, reflecting the change that will come for the family; when he overhears his father talking about Korea, the boy realises how his father feels towards him; the older generation seem to think more of themselves and money than of their children; compare with the distance between father and son in 'A Family Supper'; compare with the discovery of cruelty and violence in the older generation in 'The Darkness Out There'; compare the two narrators and their reactions in 'Korea' and 'Chemistry'.

9. *Animal Farm*
   Old Major is 'wise' and respected by the other animals so his ideas are listened to; he makes a logical and persuasive case against Man. He

sounds reasonable; his 'dream' gives an almost mystical power to his ideas; although he talks about rebellion he does not make any practical plans for it and says it might not come for a long time; he is the equivalent of V. I. Lenin, whose ideas shaped communism; he dies before the rebellion so we cannot know whether he would have remained an idealist; it is up to others to put his ideas into practice and interpret them; after the rebellion his ideas are changed and his followers corrupted; this reflects the history of the USSR and other regimes based on egalitarian ideals.

10. *Never Let Me Go*
She is a first person narrator and we see everything through her eyes; she is a naïve narrator as she does not understand a lot of what is happening; her tone is chatty, and she shares her feelings and reactions openly; she is proud of her success as a 'carer', working within the system; she herself is not quick to question but she listens to Tommy; her naïvety and lack of understanding mean that we discover things gradually with her; she forms strong emotional relationships, demonstrating her humanity.

11. *Anita and Me*
Syal describes Indian dress and food in great detail; the narrator is very aware of her 'different' culture; the visits of the aunts and uncles and Nanima bring Indian culture to Tollington; Meena is not always happy with being different and is drawn to the culture of Tollington; religion is part of the culture but is not as important to Meena's parents as to others; the stories told by her family give Meena a sense of culture, tradition and history; at the end, when they move, she embraces Indian culture and her ethnic identity more fully.

12. *Pigeon English*
The novel opens with a murder and Harrison becomes obsessed with 'the dead boy'; he witnesses the violent attack on Mr Frimpong and is drawn into a world of violent gangs; at first he is excited by violence, as if it wasn't real, but comes to understand the reality of it; there is violence in school and among teenagers outside school; Aunty Sonia has harmed herself to stay in the country; Miquita suffers violence from her boyfriend; it is a world of gangs, knives and guns – even the police on the tube are said to have guns; the climax, with Harrison himself being murdered, seems inevitable.

Pages 40–41: Poetry

For questions **1–2**, look at the mark scheme below. **[Maximum 30 marks]**

Marks	Skills
26–30 (Grade 8–9)	You have: compared texts in an exploratory and critical way; used precise, appropriate references to support your interpretation; analysed the writers' methods using subject terminology appropriately; explored the effects of the writers' methods; explored links between text and ideas/context.
21–25 (Grade 7)	You have: made thoughtful, developed comparisons; used appropriate references to support your interpretation; examined the writers' methods using subject terminology effectively; examined the effects of the writers' methods; thoughtfully considered links between text and ideas/context.
16–20 (Grade 5–6)	You have: made clear comparisons; used references effectively to support your explanation; explained the writers' methods clearly using relevant subject terminology; understood the effects of the writers' methods; clearly considered the links between text and ideas/context.
11–15 (Grade 3–4)	You have: explained your comparisons; used references to support your comments; explained some of the writers' methods using some relevant subject terminology; explained the effects of the writers' methods; made some relevant links between text and ideas/context.
6–10 (Grade 2)	You have: responded to the texts and compared them; commented on references; identified some of the writers' methods using some subject terminology; identified some effects of the writers' methods; made some links between text and ideas/context.
1–5 (Grade 1)	You have: commented on the texts; referred to some details; are aware of the writer making choices and may have used some subject terminology; attempted to comment on the effects of the writers' methods; attempted to make links between text and ideas/context.

Depending on which poem you chose to compare, your answer might include the following points.

1. • The poet associates memories with a place – 'Neutral Tones', 'Winter Swans', 'Letters from Yorkshire'.
   • Imagery of nature – 'When We Two Parted', 'Love's Philosophy', Sonnet 29, 'The Farmer's Bride', 'Winter Swans', 'Neutral Tones'.
   • Parent/child relationships – 'Follower', 'Walking Away', 'Mother, any distance', 'Before You Were Mine'.
   • Sense of another time expressed through detail – 'Before You were Mine', 'Follower', 'Walking Away'.
   • Sense of mortality – 'Neutral Tones', 'Follower'.
   • Use of natural imagery – 'Neutral Tones', 'Love's Philosophy', 'Winter Swans', 'The Farmer's Bride'.
   • Use of rhyme/half rhyme – 'Walking Away', 'Follower'.
   • Form and structure – regular quatrains with 'footnote' at the end.

2. • Account of a battle/war – 'The Charge of the Light Brigade', 'Exposure', 'Remains'.
   • Focus on suffering of individuals – 'Exposure', 'War Photographer', 'The Emigrée'.
   • The experience of the soldier – 'Exposure', 'Remains', 'Poppies', 'Kamikaze', 'The Charge of the Light Brigade'.
   • Ideas about patriotism and country – 'The Charge of the Light Brigade', 'Poppies', 'Kamikaze', 'Checking out Me History', 'Exposure'.
   • Imagery from nature – 'Exposure', 'The Prelude', 'Storm on the Island', 'Kamikaze'.
   • Death and mortality –'Remains', 'Exposure', 'War Photographer'.
   • Use of past tense – 'The Charge of the Light Brigade', 'Remains', 'Kamikaze' – contrast 'Exposure'.
   • Structure – three long stanzas, free verse – compare and contrast 'The Charge of the Light Brigade', 'Exposure', 'War Photographer', 'Remains'.

Pages 42–43: Unseen Poetry

1. **[Maximum 24 marks]**

Marks	Skills
21–24 (Grade 8–9)	You have: explored the text critically; used precise references to support your interpretation; analysed the writer's methods using appropriate subject terminology.
17–20 (Grade 7)	You have: responded thoughtfully to the text; used appropriate references to support your interpretation; examined the writer's methods using subject terminology effectively.
13–16 (Grade 5–6)	You have: responded clearly to the text; used references effectively to support your explanation; explained the writer's methods using relevant subject terminology; understood the effects of the writer's methods on the reader.
9–12 (Grade 3–4)	You have: explained your response to the text; used references to support your comments; explained some of the writer's methods using some relevant subject terminology; identified the effects of the writer's methods on the reader.
5–8 (Grade 2)	You have: responded to the text; commented on references; identified some of the writer's methods using some subject terminology; commented on the effects of the writer's methods on the reader.
1–4 (Grade 1)	You have: commented on the text; referred to some details; are aware of the writer making choices and may have used some subject terminology; attempted to comment on the effects of the writer's methods on the reader.

Your answer might include comments on:

Repetition of 'I remember, I remember' at the start of each stanza; short lines and rhyme give a childish feel to the poem; words like 'little' and 'peeping' add to the sentimental view of childhood; memories all involve literal imagery in descriptions of nature; he looks back on his childhood as a time of pure happiness; each stanza, except for the third, contrasts his happy memory with his feelings now; childhood seen from the point of view as an older, sick person; there is a lot of colour (in the second stanza) and movement (in the third), giving a sense of a child's wonder and enthusiasm for life; the regularity of metre and rhyme scheme contain his emotions, both joyful and sad; the last four lines almost dismiss childhood experience ('It was a childish ignorance') and reflect on how he has changed; he does not explain why he thinks he is 'farther off from Heaven'. What sort of life has he led?

2. [Maximum 8 marks]

Marks	Skills
7–8 (Grade 7–9)	You have made an exploratory comparison of the writers' use of language, structure and form, using accurate and appropriate subject terminology. You have convincingly compared the effects of the writers' methods on the reader.
5–6 (Grade 5–6)	You have thoughtfully compared the writers' use of language, structure and form, effectively using subject terminology. You have compared the effects of the writers' methods on the reader.
3–4 (Grade 3–4)	You have made a relevant comparison of the writers' use of language, structure and form, with some relevant use of subject terminology. You have made some comparison of the effects of the writers' methods on the reader.
1–2 (Grade 1–2)	You have made some links between the writers' use of language or structure or form. You have made some links between the effects of the writers' methods on the reader.

Your answer might include comments on:

The first is written by an older man looking back on childhood, the second from the child's point of view; when describing childhood experience, both express joy and excitement (both describing a swing); both describe nature (literal imagery): flowers, trees, cattle, etc; both seem to have safe, secure childhoods, contained in gardens; Stevenson's poem has no awareness of growing old; Stevenson's poem has a simple rhyme scheme and metre, like Hood's, but has shorter stanzas; Stevenson's sentiments are as simple as the form, unlike Hood's. It might be written for children.

English Literature Set B

Pages 45–50: Shakespeare

For all questions, look at the mark scheme for Set A, on page 77. **[Maximum 30 marks plus 4 marks for AO4]**

Your answers could include some of the following points.

1. *Macbeth*
Repetition of 'blood' shows obsession with violence; 'Our great bidding' shows his pride as king – he expects obedience; he controls the country through spies; he is 'steeped in so far' that he will not turn back; he will become more ruthless; there is a sense that he is out of control, lacking sleep and having 'strange things' in his head.

The witches' prophecy makes him think about being king; at first he is unsure and has a conscience but Lady Macbeth pushes him into murdering Duncan; the murder of Banquo and attempt to murder Fleance show his increasing paranoia and ruthlessness; strange omens are reported and Scotland suffers under his reign; the murder of Lady Macduff and her children shows a new level of cruelty.

2. *Romeo and Juliet*
Here Juliet drinks the Friar's potion to avoid marrying Paris and to be united with Romeo; the fear she shows underlines how desperate and determined she is while reminding us of her youth; her imagination runs wild,

as she contemplates the horror of waking in a tomb; her soliloquy is full of questions and caesuras, as one thought leads to another; the language is macabre and ghoulish, striking fear in the audience.

We know from the prologue that Juliet will die; Romeo and Juliet's love is doomed because of the violent feud between their families; Romeo's love for Juliet leads indirectly to the deaths of Tybalt and Mercutio; during the 'balcony' scene there are premonitions of death just as they are falling in love; the intensity of their love causes them to kill themselves; they are united in death.

3. *The Tempest*
Ferdinand plays on Miranda's name to express his admiration; he compares her to other women, judging her to be better than any he has seen; she admits that she is 'skilless' in judging men but cannot imagine anyone better; they see each other as ideals. He talks of virtues while she focuses on appearance; Ferdinand uses the word 'bondage' of love. He has just been enslaved by Prospero.

The main love relationship is between father and child, Prospero and Miranda; Miranda's only other experience of a man is Caliban, who assaulted her; elsewhere, relationships that should be based on love, between brothers, have broken down and must be mended; marriage is seen as important for reasons of politics as well as love; Miranda's innocence and purity (her 'dower') are emphasised; it is important that Ferdinand's intentions are honourable.

4. *Much Ado about Nothing*
The audience is aware of Hero and Ursula's plot to make Beatrice acknowledge her feelings; Beatrice's attempts to remain hidden (when in fact the others know she is there) provide comedy; Hero and Ursula's praise for Benedick is hyperbolic and intended for Beatrice's ears; Beatrice's closing soliloquy alerts us to her true feelings and intentions; here, trickery is used to reveal truth; in the masque, disguise allows people freedom to tell the truth; however it can also be used maliciously to deceive; Don John's trick, designed to make Claudio believe that Hero is unfaithful, works and almost causes tragedy; Claudio

is tricked into thinking Hero is dead to make him realise that he loves her; the final trick has elements of magic and religious symbolism with Hero apparently brought back to life.

5. *The Merchant of Venice*
Here Shylock is seen imprisoning his daughter so sympathy would probably be for her; the language he uses when describing the masques makes him appear a killjoy; his anti-Christian sentiments ('Christian fools', etc.) might offend audiences; his stated intention to sack Lancelot makes him unsympathetic; however, Jessica's couplet at the end of the scene indicates that his fears for her are justified; consider the likely differences between Elizabethan and modern audience sympathies; audience sympathies are likely to be with Jessica when she elopes but might shift when Shylock hears about what she has done; when he insists on the 'pound of flesh' in court, audiences might be repelled; however, their sympathies might shift when he is humiliated at the end.

6. *Julius Caesar*
Brutus and Cassius are equal partners and both leaders. Here, cracks begin to show in their relationship; Cassius appears sensitive about his position – the 'wrong' is that he feels 'slighted'; Brutus is concerned more with ethics: Cassius should not have interfered with justice on behalf of a friend; Brutus accuses Cassius of having an 'itching palm', making the argument more personal; this brings a violent reaction from Cassius; Brutus takes the moral high ground, asserting that they killed Caesar for the sake of justice; Brutus's 'noble' reputation is important to Cassius as it attracts support for the conspiracy; their personalities are very different. Cassius is more pragmatic and wily; in spite of this they admire each other and have a warm friendship, shown when they make up after this argument, using affectionate language.

Pages 51–57: The 19th Century Novel

Look at the mark scheme for Set A, on page 77.
[Maximum 30 marks plus 4 marks for AO4]

Your answers could include some of the following points.

1. *The Strange Case of Dr Jekyll and Mr Hyde*
The description of the scene at twilight creates a sad, gentle mood; Jekyll is compared to a 'disconsolate prisoner', making him seem like a victim; Jekyll's words about being 'low' and it 'will not last long' suggest an illness he is not in control of; Jekyll is polite and pleasant when speaking to the visitors; the sudden change in his look is frightening and the 'terror and despair' is like the reaction of a victim; Jekyll is discussed by Utterson and Lanyon as someone who used to be a good, reasonable man but has become strange; his friends are inclined to see him as a victim of Hyde and want to help him; Dr Lanyon's narrative

reveals the full horror of what Jekyll has become and his 'moral turpitude'; Jekyll's own narrative gives us insight into his motives and his feelings about what he has done, making him sympathetic again.

2. *A Christmas Carol*
The Cratchits show their love for Tim and for each other after the 'death' of Tiny Tim; Mrs Cratchit is anxious about Bob, not thinking of herself; Bob tries to be positive, speaking of the 'green place' where Tim is to be buried, but breaks down; contrast between reactions to Scrooge's death and Tiny Tim's; the reaction of Scrooge's nephew contrasts with how Scrooge treats people including the Cratchits; the Cratchits represent decent hard-working people who find it hard to get by; they are the model of a loving, cheerful family, and show the true spirit of Christmas; Scrooge's treatment of Bob shows him to be a bad employer, in contrast with his old boss Fezziwig; Scrooge learns from watching the Cratchits at home. Their home life is the opposite of his; sending the turkey to the Cratchits shows how much Scrooge has changed.

3. *Great Expectations*
The setting in the graveyard makes Magwitch's first appearance terrifying and memorable; he is described as an intimidating figure and is clearly an escaped convict but his cold and hunger might make him sympathetic; his speech, rough both in content and style, is in stark contrast to Pip's; although frightening to young Pip, there is a comic element to the character brought out by the adult narrator; his physical strength is emphasised.

He is absent for most of the novel and not even mentioned so that his reappearance comes as a surprise; Pip's reaction to discovering he is his benefactor puts Pip in an unsympathetic light – he mentions his 'abhorrence'; in contrast to Pip and his 'expectations', Magwitch has done well through his own hard work; Magwitch tells his own story, making him sympathetic and correcting a lot of Pip's misunderstandings; the fact that he could turn Pip into a gentleman – and that he is Estella's father – questions the idea of social class and privilege; he is like a father to Pip and Pip comes to see that he is a 'better man'.

4. *Jane Eyre*
Jane is included in the party but sits apart, listening, and not making a contribution; she slips out by a side-door, wanting to be as unobtrusive as possible; Rochester seems concerned about her but questions her abruptly; he also gives her orders, 'Return to the drawing-room'; she is conscious of not having the 'freedom' to speak to him as an equal; she is from an upper or upper-middle class background but is impoverished and has to earn a living; her position means that she can mix with (and observe) servants as well as employers and their friends; she does not like the affectations of people like the snobbish Ingrams; her judgments are not based on

class – she can praise or condemn people regardless of their background; Rochester does not care about her class or background; ultimately, though, she returns to her 'proper' position in life, getting an inheritance as well as a 'good' marriage.

5. *Frankenstein*
   Frankenstein compares his enthusiasm to a 'hurricane' and there is a sense of violent haste about the account; he admits that pride and ambition motivate him; there is a sense of the virtue of pursuing knowledge, bringing 'a torrent of light into our dark world'; however, his language betrays a desire to 'play God' by becoming a 'creator'; his description of the 'horrors' of his work, digging up bones, etc., conveys a sense of revulsion at odds with his ideas about doing something noble; this is seen as 'profane', against religion and God, in desecrating holy ground.

   After giving the creature life, Frankenstein is instantly repelled and rejects his creation; he makes no attempt to care for or educate the creature, which therefore has to learn from its experience; he becomes afraid of the creature and remorseful about his actions; he is punished for his act of creation by the deeds of the creature and his own misery.

6. *Pride and Prejudice*
   Austen describes Mr Collins's reaction ironically by using the kind of hyperbolic vocabulary he might have used – 'triumph', 'grandeur'; his 'triumph' depends on others ('his wondering visitors') being as snobbish; Sir William responds in the same way, showing off about his own 'situation in life', to assert his superiority to Mr Collins; Mr Collins assumes others will be as impressed as he is and keen that the experience does not 'overpower' them, the implication being that he hopes it does; his advice to Elizabeth about her dress is comic because of its inappropriateness – as a man he would not be expected to discuss such things with ladies; snobbery is shown by his concern with superficial things like how people dress and how many rooms they have; what he says about Lady Catherine and the 'distinction of rank' proves to be true, showing that she is a snob; Darcy is also a snob, though not as obviously as his aunt. This is shown in his behaviour at the Meryton ball; Jane's romance with Bingley is almost ruined by the snobbery of Darcy and Bingley's sisters; perhaps Elizabeth might also be a bit of a snob. Consider her feelings about her family's behaviour at Netherfield Park.

7. *The Sign of Four*
   Watson is excited about showing the treasure to Miss Morston and proud of being allowed to bring it; he may see the treasure as proof of his love for her; she has 'no eagerness in her voice', surprising us by her apparent 'indifference' to the treasure; tension and expectation are built by the description of the box and the difficulty of opening it; the treasure box is exotic and incongruous in Mrs Forrester's house, the use of Mrs Forrester's poker adding some humour; as soon as he sees the box is empty Watson feels relieved. The treasure was a 'golden barrier' between him and Miss Morston; the fact that she feels the same proves their mutual love; finding the treasure seemed to be the point of the adventure but solving the mystery and finding out the truth are more important; the pursuit of it has placed Holmes, Watson and others in 'horrible peril'; it is the motive for the killing of Jonathan Sholto and the reason for the death of Morston; the story of Jonathan Small shows that the Agra treasure – or rather the desire of people to possess it – has always caused unhappiness and death.

Pages 58–61: Modern Prose or Drama

Look at the mark scheme for Set A on page 77.
[Maximum 30 plus 4 marks for AO4]

Your answers could include some of the following points.

1. *An Inspector Calls*
   The Inspector takes charge and commands respect; he is an 'outsider' and does not belong to the world the Birlings move in; he acts like a detective in that he is investigating something and asking a lot of questions; he is not really investigating a crime but is looking into the reasons for Eva's act; he apportions blame and judges the other characters; he moralises about society and warns of the consequences of acting like the Birlings; his name, Goole, is pronounced the same as 'ghoul'. Is he a ghost from the future?; he has come from the 1940s, the time the play was written, to examine an earlier time; he may be warning the audience not to return to the society of 1912; he can be seen as the voice of the writer.

2. *Blood Brothers*
   Linda stands up for Mickey to his brother and the other older children; she is one of the gang, equal to the boys in their games; she is protective and caring towards Mickey; the conversation about dying prefigures the end of the play, as does Sammy's gun; she is pragmatic in a comic childish way: 'if y'dead, there's no school'; here Mickey introduces Linda to Edward for the first time: their relationship will be crucial; in the park Linda proves better than the boys at shooting: is Russell making a feminist point?; she is outgoing and witty, and she helps to create a lighter atmosphere as she and the boys have fun together; she is in love with Mickey but, as his wife, is frustrated in her attempts to help him; she turns to Edward for help, unwittingly bringing the tragedy closer.

3. *The History Boys*
   Mrs Lintott says Posner wants to know if Irwin has 'ceased to be a teacher and become a friend', implying you cannot be both; Posner is looking for personal advice, which could be seen as part of a teacher's job; Irwin seeks to discover more about Hector's relationship with the boys; this could be seen as crossing a professional line or as showing concern about Hector

crossing lines; Posner notices Irwin's interest in Dakin. Dakin takes advantage of this attraction and treats Irwin as if he were a friend; Hector blurs the lines between teacher/pupil relationships and friendship. Even without the 'groping' he could be seen as over-friendly; it could be said that a 'friendly' relationship with pupils is helpful in teaching but that is not the same as becoming friends; at times the friendship between staff and pupils can seem fun and positive but it can also be harmful and manipulative (on both sides).

4. *DNA*
They do not seem to have made any moral choice about the 'killing'. Things just got out of control; however, the act shows an inability to apply a sense of right and wrong; led by Phil, they make the choice to blame someone else for their actions; Leah talks about the bonobos and having empathy: empathy might be the closest they get to morality, but they do not usually apply it; they are concerned with self-preservation and will do anything to avoid getting into trouble; Lou and Danny have doubts about framing the postman but their concerns are mostly about the effect on them of being found out; towards the end, several characters suffer under the weight of guilt, e.g. Brian 'on medication', John Tate disappearing; at the end Leah tries to stand up for the truth but is not listened to and ends up leaving; the ending is bleak, with no sense of justice being done; at best their morality is relative. Some might say that, as a group, they were amoral.

5. *The Curious Incident of the Dog in the Night-Time*
Christopher is concerned by the fact that he has been accused of killing Wellington; he like facts and is not willing to let this go – he needs to know the truth; he applies his own logic to the case, based on dogs being as important as people; Ed's reaction suggests to the audience (but not to literal-minded Christopher) that he is hiding something; his investigation will lead him to uncover the truth about other things, like his parents' marriage; he becomes more independent, taking the initiative and facing his fears, e.g. on the train; other characters may begin to value him more, but does he value them more?; he himself attributes his increased confidence and success to the incident: 'I can because I went to London on my own.'; we are left wondering how much he can achieve ('Does that mean I can do anything?'); how much has he changed? And if he has not changed, does it matter?

6. *A Taste of Honey*
In the extract Jo seems unconcerned about how she will manage, as Geof questions her about money; she shows her immaturity and lack of understanding of what motherhood will mean; her attitude might be a way of avoiding her true feelings; she does not say she wants to be a mother but refuses to consider abortion; she says she does not know much about love – will she be able to love the baby?; Geof, not knowing her, assumes Helen will care because she is Jo's mother; later she panics and says 'I don't want to be a mother';

Geof tries to help her but she reacts by joking and flirting, trying to avoid the subject of motherhood; Helen's idea of being a mother is unconventional. She is selfish and shows little concern for Jo; she becomes sentimental about the baby but focuses on material things like the cot; their love–hate relationship is the central one in both their lives.

7. *Lord of the Flies*
Being British is a shorthand for being civilised; the boys' ideas of correct behaviour are entwined with ideas about being British, learned at home and at public school; the officer talks about British boys putting on a 'better show'. Being British means coping with adversity; at the time the novel was written, Britain's place in the world was changing, the days of Empire coming to an end; the sense of 'Britishness' alluded to by the officer is a male upper class concept; the novel is influenced by the kind of boys' adventure stories popular in the 19th and early 20th centuries, in which British boys overcame danger and adversity; Britain is associated with colonialism – the events of the novel undermine the idea of colonialism; Golding implicitly criticises all nation states, not just Britain, and their involvement in wars.

8. *Telling Tales*
At the beginning, stories about crashed planes and girls being attacked are just rumours to Sandra, not reality; her walk to the cottage in the woods is reminiscent of a fairy tale; Mrs Rutter's story reveals the reality of war and death; the young people are shocked at how Mrs Rutter and her sister behaved; she sees Kerry differently because of his angry reaction: 'older and larger'; she feels that her life is changed and sees the 'darkness out there'; compare with the way in which the narrator learns about death and growing up in 'Chemistry'; compare with the change in the narrator's feelings about his father in 'Korea'; compare the change to Elizabeth's life in 'The Odour of Chrysanthemums'.

9. *Animal Farm*
Old Major blames humans for all the animals' problems; he states that 'we must not come to resemble them' and lists things that animals must never do; even when they are putting up the commandments, the pigs give instructions to the other animals; the pigs learn human skills and take privileges for themselves but Squealer stops opposition by threatening the return of humans; they breed dogs to keep order and they follow Napoleon as they did Mr Jones; the pigs start dealing with humans, using money and sleeping at the farmhouse, but have an answer for every criticism; the other animals change from being willing comrades and supporters to being confused and questioning, but they continue to obey the pigs; the pigs eventually rule by terror and are more cruel than humans; at the end the pigs are indistinguishable from men, their transformation complete; these changes reflect the changes in the behaviour of leaders in communist and other populist regimes.

10. *Never Let Me Go*

Ruth voices her feelings about being a clone, which no-one else has articulated; the word 'clone' is rarely used in the novel and for a long time the reader might not realise the characters are clones; Ruth feels that the others are living a fantasy, trying to make themselves feel better; she associates clones with 'trash' – they are even less than the worst humans; Kathy has hinted at their origins before and they may be right; in spite of the clones knowing that they are different, they have human emotions and human relationships; Kathy feels that their 'human' behaviour is learned, with her friends imitating relationships and behaviour they see on television; at the end her feelings are no different from the feeling of any human; we see everything through a clone's eyes, leading us to wonder what the difference is between clones and humans; we might ask whether it will be possible to create clones in this way and, if so, will they feel and think like humans?

11. *Anita and Me*

The house is described as old-fashioned and uncomfortable; Meena's father gets 'sick of it' and its distance from work; Tollington's situation in the countryside appeals to Meena's mother; she likes it because it reminds her of home in the Punjab; she is seen as unusual and odd by other Indians who want modern houses nearer the city; Tollington itself is a poor run-down village; part of its appeal to the young Meena is its size and the sense of community; the family is conscious of being the only Indian family and therefore the object of curiosity and prejudice; they are also middle class and better educated than most of their neighbours and they sometimes look down on them; as Meena gets older, she becomes more aware of racism and the differences between her and other Tollington people.

12. *Pigeon English*

Mamma is a dominant character in Harrison's life; she is seen as hard-working and caring, perhaps a stereotypical African mother; Aunty Sonia is a more disturbing figure. She is entertaining and fascinating but her self-harm is disturbing; Lydia is a stereotypical older sister, fighting with Harrison and bossing him around; his crush on Poppy gives some relief from the violence; women, such as Miquita and Aunty Sonia, are seen as victims of violence; although they are portrayed as strong personalities, they are largely ineffective; the gangs depicted are all male and the violence is mostly done by males; adult males, if not violent or criminal, do not feature much in Harrison's life.

Pages 62–63: Poetry

For questions 1–2, look at the mark scheme for Set A, Poetry on page 81. **[Maximum 30 marks]**

Depending on which poem you chose to compare, your answer might include some of the following points.

1. • Literal imagery: the poet describes the weather – 'Neutral Tones', 'When We Two Parted, 'Eden Rock', 'The Farmer's Bride'.

• Pathetic fallacy as weather reflects mood – 'When We Two Parted', 'Neutral Tones', 'Porphyria's Lover'.

• Pathetic fallacy in nature having human attributes ('gulping for breath') – 'Love's Philosophy'.

• A real event remembered – 'Eden Rock', 'Walking Away', 'Mother, any distance', 'Before You Were Mine'.

• Observing nature makes the poet consider his relationship – 'Love's Philosophy', 'Neutral Tones', 'Follower', 'Walking Away'.

• Intensity of feeling expressed by imagery – Sonnet 29, 'Love's Philosophy', 'When We Two Parted'.

• Literal imagery of the swans becomes extended metaphor for relationship – 'Neutral Tones'.

• Form and structure – six three-line stanzas and a final two-line stanza, giving a sense of brief impressionistic memories – 'Eden Rock', 'Neutral Tones'.

• Final short stanza brings a conclusion.

2. • Experience of a battle/war – 'The Charge of the Light Brigade', 'Exposure', 'Bayonet Charge'.

• First person account of a life-changing experience – 'The Prelude', 'Exposure'.

• Poet adopts a persona – 'My Last Duchess'.

• Poem based on reports/research not personal experience – 'The Charge of the Light Brigade', 'Bayonet Charge', 'War Photographer', contrast 'Exposure'.

• Colloquial style conveying sense of conversation – 'Exposure'.

• Individual haunted and shaped by memory – 'War Photographer', 'The Emigrée', 'The Prelude'.

• Violent imagery and diction – 'Exposure', 'Bayonet Charge', 'War Photographer'.

• The effect of war on individuals – 'Bayonet Charge', 'Poppies', 'War Photographer', 'Kamikaze'.

• Use of present tense, showing how the past is still alive – 'Exposure', contrast 'Bayonet Charge', 'The Charge of the Light Brigade'.

• Structure – stanzas of equal length, varied line length followed by final one of two lines.

• No regular metre or rhyme scheme but some rhyme and half rhyme used – 'Exposure', 'Storm on the Island'.

Pages 64–65: Unseen Poetry

1. Look at the mark scheme for Set A, Unseen Poetry on page 82. **[Maximum 24 marks]**

Your answer might include comments on:

Comparison of frost to a ghost sets mood and makes us think of death; depressing mood continues with language like 'dregs', 'desolate' and 'weakening'; landscape and weather reflects poet's mood – pathetic fallacy; in the second stanza Hardy places himself in the landscape; he associates the landscape with passing time, the century (19th) coming to an end; uses an extended metaphor of a corpse, continuing morbid theme; use of alliteration of hard 'c' gives a sharp, uncomfortable tone; there is a sudden change ('At once') with the sound of the thrush; contrast of the 'joy' of the thrush with the death-like landscape; religious imagery in 'evensong', 'soul' and 'carolings'; the age and weakness of the thrush makes his singing more extraordinary; Hardy sees the thrush as making an active choice to 'fling his soul'; the poet is unaware of the 'blessed Hope' but the thrush's song shows him the possibility of hope.

2. **Look at the mark scheme for Set A Unseen Poetry on page 83. [Maximum 8 marks]**

Your answer might include comments on:

In both of them the poet is alone in the landscape; the landscape and weather are harsh in both, reflecting the poets' moods; in 'The Darkling Thrush' the poet's mood is changed but in 'Spellbound' it remains the same; Brontë does not say what the 'tyrant spell' is, whether it is from nature or her own feelings. Similarly, Hardy does not explain his mood; Hardy writes about an incident in the past – Brontë writes in the present tense; Brontë's natural imagery is literal and simple, while Hardy uses an elaborate extended metaphor in the second stanza, as well as a simile in the first stanza; Brontë uses repetition and a refrain to give a sense of her situation; at first Brontë seems powerless but the last line suggests she is choosing to be where she is ('I will not'); while the weather depresses Hardy and his mood is rescued by the thrush, Brontë seems to rejoice in the 'dreary' night; both poems are regular in form and structure.